Love, Life & Lessons Learned

Collection of Inspirational Stories From
Women Authentically Sharing Lessons Learned
About Life And Love.

Ann L. Esters-Stevenson

Dedication

This book is dedicated to my parents, Edward &
Geraldine {Gerrie} Ann Esters. Thank you for loving me
beyond what any heart could measure by both saying it and
showing it. Your guidance and the values you instilled in me
is what caused this book to come to fruition. The love you
both effortlessly gave me throughout my entire life, coupled
with life's lessons along the way, have made me the woman I
am today. I Pray I've made you proud. I love you. I miss you
& I can't wait for us to see each other again in the heavenly
realm.

Table of Contents

Acknowledgements

To my wonderful Husband, Shaun L. Stevenson, thank you for your role in my finally experiencing what real love feels like. The love you've shown me is immeasurable. You've been my rock when I felt like throwing in the towel. You've been my leader at times when I was lost and didn't know what to do. Most important, you've been my prayer partner praying for me like no other when I felt like I couldn't push through. Thank you my Love for going on this journey with me as we stand in unison to make a difference in the lives we'll continue to touch through our Love, our Life, and our Lessons Learned.

To my siblings, my family, my 2 best friends, and of course my fur baby, Seven, thank you for your overall repetitive support and continuous prayers coupled with your silence at times to just extend a listening ear. Thank you for encouraging me to take this leap of faith and making me feel empowered to do so. There are lessons to be learned for all of us as it relates to family and friendships. I'm thankful to each of you for loving me unconditionally and believing in me as I embark upon what God has pre-destined for my next-next.

To the amazingly beautiful co-authors who gave of yourselves so unselfishly to pour into the lives of our readers,

I salute you. It's not easy to come to terms with emotions that are experienced as it relates to love, forgiveness, hurt, betrayal, and self-esteem throughout life and as a result, it can be just as difficult to accept any lessons learned. You are a pillar in gaining souls for the Kingdom of God. I'm in awe of you and so extremely humbled at your willingness to serve God by sharing the very fabric of your souls exposing what some would deem our vulnerabilities. Quite the contrary. I deem you as a woman who is the epitome of strength, dignity, and grace! I Love You! I Really Do!

And most important, I would like to thank God for giving up his only Son for me. I am grateful for who He is and who He has been in my life. God, You are my everything and I know that I know (that I know), you have my back, my front, my sides, and my corners. With you, I know that all things are possible and I thank you for reminding me of exactly who I am, who I belong to, and who you called me to be. You are the epitome of Love. You gave me Life and the Lessons I've learned just based on my relationship with you makes me want to shout! I Love You! I Honor You! And, I Adore You!

Foreword

We all have a story or stories to tell. When you think of the title "Love, Life, & Lessons Learned," I am sure several things come rushing to mind. Some, that as you reflect, may make you smile, laugh out loud, feel a little sad, or stir a bit of anger. You may have even felt a *"Listen, let me tell you!"* rise up within you. When I sat down to write the foreword for this book, I thought to myself, where do I begin? I have so much to say on the topic(s) of love, life, and the lessons they bring. No one has more stories on this than me trust me. But the single most important thing I could say about the journey throughout life and all of its lessons, is the stories you've racked up are never about you; they are about the lives you could change and the souls you could possibly set free out of your experiences. I am the poster child for turning pain into purpose. I know what it means to win and lose only to win again, and then take every up and down, and twist and turn of life's accounts and mold them into beautiful teachable moments for others to glean from. It is for this reason I feel so connected to this project and to the visionary, Ann Esters-Stevenson. Ann has proven, genuine, concern for women's awareness when it comes to loving, valuing, and caring for themselves and equally as important, one another. We share the same vision when it comes to wanting to see people win in life and make the best out of life whether it is the one they were given, the one that betrayed them, or the one they had to create after everything fell apart.

As a church member, a co-author in my anthology, "Soul Talk," an ambassador for the Cheryl Polote-Williamson brand, as a dear friend and co-collaborator in life, I have witnessed firsthand Ann's love for God and for the people he's placed in her life. I have watched her kind and giving nature evolve into a catalyst for change in the lives of others, guiding them into knowledge of self-love and self-appreciation. I have watched the works of her hands point back to our Heavenly Father and all of His goodness. Now, it brings me great joy to support her as she endeavors to bring all of those attributes together; giving life and light to captivating personal stories of "Love, Life, and Lessons Learned" from the hearts of women who seek to provide a road map that leads from loving God; to proper love of self; to healthy, lasting relationships. Ann is producing the "Love, Life, and Lessons Learned" anthology, as is evidenced in all she does, because she wants to change lives and help people learn to love—GOD first, themselves second, then others. Prepare for a level of truth that will cause you to reflect, reveal, reconsider, redirect, transform, heal, develop, grow, and feel compelled to not only teach, but show others about "Love, Life, and Lessons Learned."

Cheryl Polote-Willilamson

Speaker

Global Leader and Entrepreneur

Award-winning Best-Selling Author

CEO & Founder – Cheryl Polote-Williamson, LLC

CEO & Founder – Williamson Media Group, LLC

Chapter 1

Redemptive Love

Tanya Bakari

"Let the redeemed of the Lord tell their story—those he redeemed from the hand of the foe." Psalm 107:2

It's been 9 years since I experienced what I considered one of the darkest seasons of my life. I didn't know how I would get through it; all I knew was that I couldn't give up. I couldn't walk away and just give it all to Satan. There was too much on the line; too much at stake. While in my heart, I felt that way, my mind swung like a pendulum between fear, faith, and fight. One moment, I was faith-filled, and then not! I had never been this way before, so it was difficult to wrap my mind around how to one, stop the madness; two, stand and fight; and three, walk in faith. But I told God that I would not be ashamed…WHEN HE restored it all; that I would tell my story.

It was Friday, July 17, 2009. We were celebrating our 13th wedding anniversary. We got dressed and went to dinner in Dallas; although this was a momentous occasion, there was something off about the whole evening. We didn't talk much and certainly didn't seem to be in a celebratory mood. We went to dinner and went home. The next day, my husband went out with a friend to provide support for him, as he was dealing with difficulty in his marriage. I didn't think too much of it; however, Sunday morning, he informed me he wouldn't be attending church that day, which was unusual. I couldn't shake the feeling that something was wrong; so on my way to church, I called him and he was inattentive and cold. I made the statement, "You act like you don't want this anymore." With a long pause and what felt like an eternity of silence, he responded, "You're right, I don't." I couldn't believe what I was hearing, so I said, "You're saying you don't want to be married anymore?" His immediate response was "Yes, I don't want this anymore."

At that moment in time, everything slowed down. As I pulled up to the church, tears fell slowly down my cheeks. This was a pain and a hurt that I had never experienced, and I didn't know what to do with it. I got out and walked toward the church quietly and subtly attempting to pull myself together, but it was beyond my control. My heart felt as though it had been punched with a force greater than I could bear. During the whole service, my focus was off, all I could do was replay that conversation in my head. After church, I went home knowing that this was only the beginning of a fight that I didn't understand how to fight.

Upon arriving home, he and I talked and I can see it as if it were yesterday. He sat on the foot of our bed and told me he was not in love with me anymore and didn't want the marriage anymore. All I could do was look at him, but then I got the courage to ask why? And he informed me he was just not happy. Let me ask a question, what do you do when someone tells you that they are not in love with you anymore and aren't happy? I hope you know because at that moment I did not; however, hopefully as I share my story with you, it will be revealed and you will walk away understanding how to respond. 1 Corinthians 13:13 states, "Three things will last forever—faith, hope, and love—and the greatest of these is love." But, at that moment, not one scripture surfaced in my mind. I was dumbfounded. Those words pierced my heart like a hot dagger. My husband and I had weathered a lot of storms and we always came out on top. We had one another's backs and he always treated me like a Queen; so where was this coming from and why?

Let's flashback to the year 2007. We were at church, and there was a guest speaker. She shared with my husband and me that his purpose would be birthed through me. Neither one of us understood what that meant; however, I took it to mean that whatever it was, he was about to BLOW UUUUP! You see, my husband is an entrepreneur at heart. He was building a name in the real-estate world, so I thought my job was to continue to push him and pray so that we could amass all the stuff and the lifestyle we were working towards.

As a result, we continued to pursue that lifestyle and packed all of our stuff; and we moved to a beautiful home, purchased new cars, and traveled. We were living the life; so we thought. Then the mortgage industry took a turn for the worse and we lost everything. Even with losing everything and moving our family from a 4000 square foot home to a 900 square foot apartment, we were still alright. At least, I thought we were. We continued to serve dutifully in the church; we were faithful givers of our time, talent and treasure. We looked the part of a happy couple, in spite of our circumstances.

We had been in that little 900 square foot apartment two years when we hit that wall and at that moment, the world I once knew began to crumble. I had given notice at my job, where I had quickly climbed the ladder and was on the fast track to becoming an officer in the company. All because we had agreed that I would leave and build upon a business opportunity that had proven to yield successful results. So I quit my job; I got this news, and then in September we separated.

I took a job that October, making half the salary that I was making; working longer and more strenuous hours. I was losing weight rapidly; so much so, that the woman who had trained me during the first weeks of employment, saw me a few weeks later and asked me, "Are you alright? You look sick." I thought to myself "Wow, she is bold." I answered, "No, I'm good. Just going through something right now." That was the grace of God because typically I would have responded real fly! So she made it that day.

I found myself on many days in the inventory room, hiding behind boxes as I worked crying and praying. This was hard! And then it happened. God spoke to me and told me to "Be like those who through faith and patience inherit the promises of God"(Hebrews 6:12). This meant it was time to stop feeling sorry for myself and get to work; which was exactly what I did. I started attending counseling for myself and for my healing. I started fasting and praying and I was prepared to do whatever I needed to do to win, but it wasn't up to me. My husband is a strong-willed man and I knew that if his mind was made up, there was nothing that I could do or say to convince him otherwise, BUT! I wasn't going to just bow out and not speak my mind.

I was bold. Something that had been lost over the years. Not because of any abuse, but because I didn't realize that I wasn't happy either. I had begun to shrink into a world of introversion and seclusion. Not really sharing my opinion or thoughts on too much; just "going along to get along," as they say. In my boldness, I called my husband and told him that he was making the biggest mistake of his life and he would regret it. I told him that I wasn't giving up and he could, but it would be on him and not me. I told him that he wasn't going to be happy until he saw another man raising his children. I was angry and I was going to fight until the end and leave it all on the field; so I had to be honest and say what I was feeling. He didn't say much, he was actually very quiet.

I continued to attend my weekly counseling sessions with a woman that I hold dear to my heart, Pastor Jessie Ruffin; she quickly became more than a counselor to me. But, what I loved about her was she was real and she didn't mince words. She told me about me; prayed for me and with me; and taught me how to fight and equipped me for the Spiritual battle that I was in. She told me that I was brilliant and that I would regain employment with an employer that would afford me the ability to use my mind and that is exactly what eventually happened. The assignments that she gave me built me up and challenged me to embrace who God had created me to be.

She gave me direction and I not only took the direction but acted upon them and did what was instructed. I prayed and cried a lot, but I never gave up. God made me a promise, that He would do a quick work in my husband. There were days that I was angry and tired and at my wit's end, but I couldn't give up. One day, I was so upset that I sent my Pastor's wife a text and asked, "Can I divorce him?" Till this day, she has not responded. This wasn't what I signed up for. Our marriage was to be lived out like a fairy tale and not this nightmare that I was living.

While in counseling, working a laborious job, and fighting for my marriage; I still walked in the position of his wife. Although we were separated, I didn't want to deprive him of seeing his sons. Before I would go to work and work 12-hour shifts, I would cook and leave him a plate on the stove and tell him to come by to see the boys. I wasn't trying to play games, and I wasn't going to abort my position.

As time progressed, he saw the changes in me and asked about counseling for himself. I gave him the process and trusted him to do what was needed. I didn't want to be pushy, so I didn't ask a lot of questions. I continued to pray for him daily. He did decide to go to counseling and shared that he had made his appointment. On the day of his first session, I sent him a text to see if he was still going? I'm so glad that I did because he said that he wasn't going to go, but when he got the text he decided to go.

We continued to attend counseling and during one of my sessions Pastor Jessie said, "Your husband is going to speak into men; he is going to challenge them from a real place and ignite change, but he can't come home until he makes Jesus Christ the Lord over his life; until he puts him before everything else." A few days later, he and I were on the phone; we talked for three hours like teenagers and he said, "Baby I'm scared; I know that I can't come home until I make Jesus the head of my life." I couldn't believe what I was hearing; I had just heard those same words earlier in the week! I began to encourage him and to let him know that I was there and God's got him; God's got us.

This season seemed to feel like an eternity. We had been separated for a couple of months now, and his birthday was fast approaching; but again, I wasn't aborting my position. Birthdays were always a big deal in our home. So, I asked him to dinner and gave him his gifts. He was shocked. He said, "You still bought me gifts?" I said, "Yes, it's still your birthday." Little did I know that this would set in motion those things that God had promised. This was December

7th, 2009. My husband moved back home that weekend and he didn't just move back in, he followed the directive of his counselor, Pastor Jerry Ruffin. He called the boys into the room, got down on one knee, held my hand and looked into my eyes and asked, "Will you please forgive me for hurting you and hurting our family; for putting us through this?" He then called the boys over, while still on one knee, and asked each of them the same question.

We then began marriage counseling, and before we began, Pastor Jerry Ruffin looked at him and asked him a series of questions that were so bold, and so poignant that it demonstrated my husband's new nature. He had not only surrendered to Christ and submitted God, but to this man to ensure that he was accountable and committed to continuing to be broken before God so that he could continue to become the man God called him to be.

From that point forward, we committed to being transparent with one another, to communicate even when it was difficult. We completed our counseling assignments together, began to explore the depths of our relationship and began to date and get to know one another on a different level. We allowed God to remove all the walls; to pluck up every bitter root and create a new thing for us.

A few weeks later, our counselors informed us that we were ready for our last session and that they had never had a couple reach this point so quickly. We each had our last sessions, which were individual because we needed to lay everything down before God, to never pick it up again.

We left that season equipped to stand, to kneel, to fight, all because of the covenant. The covenant that God blessed us with when He first gave it all for us. The covenant that we made with God when we stood before Him to pronounce our lifelong love through marriage.

That season was tough. I had never been in a fight like that before and I wouldn't wish it on anyone. It is hard to hear that you're not loved and to feel as though you're expendable all because of the lack of happiness. While tough, it taught us a lot. First of all, happiness is fleeting. We can't lay our foundation on the concept of happiness, because it sets us up for failure. We have to lay our foundation in that unspeakable joy that comes from God or we will waiver and be unstable in everything we do. We have to persevere just as God's Word tells us, "Let perseverance finish its work so that you may be mature and complete, not lacking anything. If any of you lacks wisdom, you should ask God, who gives generously to all without finding fault, and it will be given to you. But when you ask, you must believe and not doubt, because the one who doubts is like a wave of the sea, blown and tossed by the wind. That person should not expect to receive anything from the Lord. Such a person is double-minded and unstable in all they do" (James 1:4-8).

Without knowing or understanding what I was doing, just by trusting God when He spoke to me that day at work, I cried and still continued to pray. Trust works. God redeemed our marriage. He didn't allow anything to destroy that which He had put together, not even us. He proved to be just who He is in my life, our lives. I won't ever forget, "The Lord God is my strength [my source of courage, my invincible army]; He has made my feet [steady and sure] like hinds' feet And makes me walk [forward with spiritual confidence] on my [a]high places [of challenge and responsibility]" (Habakkuk 3:19).

We moved from that 900 square foot apartment into a beautiful home in April of 2011. In 2012, something even more amazing happened. Remember when I shared that we were told through prophecy that my husband's purpose would be birthed through me? Well, in 2012 my husband called me at work. I was now working for a bank and using my mind to solve problems versus long days of back and knee pain, nevertheless, I digress. My husband called me to tell me that it was time. Time to do what God called him to do, plant a church.

We then began to work towards that call; collectively, in stride and in unison. We were on the same page and walking in total agreement. September 2014, Victory Church was birthed and the Lead Pastor is Aalim T. Bakari!

Had someone told me 23 years ago that I would be married to a Pastor, I would have laughed at them; however, that is exactly what had been written. Long before we met, God had a plan and none of what we endured did He waste. Romans 8:28 tells us that God uses all things for the good of those who love Him and are called according to His purpose. That is exactly what He is doing. God is using every tear we have shed; every pain to minister to His people and to draw people to Christ.

This is not a story about a marriage gone wrong, but about the redemptive power of Christ and the love God has shown us through His sacrifice. When I was going through, God made me take my eyes off me and place them ever so careful on Him. He made me get out of my comfort zone and get uncomfortable; but all the while He was equipping, orchestrating, and completing what He had started. Remember that the Bible tells us that God is faithful to finish what He has started.

Life is full of hard lessons and hopefully, we learn from them; but we have to remember this... no matter what we go through, what we endure, we can't do it without Love. It is the driving force that compels us to trust, obey and to forgive. Not because the person deserves it, but because we didn't deserve it either. Christ still took our place because

He knew that without Him, we couldn't share our Love, Life, and Lessons Learned.

I truly hope and pray that this small glimpse into the window of my life encourages and helps you. Remember that you don't have to ever do it alone. Go to God, seek wise counsel, and be willing to lay it all down. One thing I know personally is, you can only be helped to the degree that which you are willing to be transparent. What that means is you have nothing to lose, so be honest with yourself, and about your situation and find someone you can trust that can hold your hand; pray and push you to that victorious life so that you can experience Redemptive love.

If that is you, pray this prayer with me:

Dear Lord, meet me right here where I am. I can't do this by myself. I need you and want to experience redemption for myself. I give every situation over to you and I'm fully confident that you can restore what is perceived to be lost or dead in my life. Help me to take my eyes and my mind off my circumstances and place my hope in you. In Christ's name, I pray, Amen.

When you find yourself flailing in the wind and feeling like you're drowning, remember that Christ is that lifeline and He can save you. Also, remember that nothing takes God by surprise. He already knows. When I was going through counseling, one of the scriptural passages that I had to commit to memory was Psalms 139: 1-24. To this day, I still recall it when I'm going through a tough or "faith building day," as we like to call them. It's something comforting about knowing that before one day of my life had passed, God already had written my plan...your plan...our plan.

I leave you with this. We celebrated 22 years of marriage on July 17, 2018, and we are madly in love. Not because we are perfect people, but because we have learned to love the imperfections. God is able to restore and redeem whatever is dead in your life. For you, it may not be a marriage, it could be an estranged relationship with a child, parent, or friend. Whatever it is, give it to God and ask Him to work on you as He works through you. Redemption is not just for one, but is a gift offered to all, so why not accept that gift?

Redemptive Love Lessons Learned
Key Points

1. **Trust God Through It All**

   It doesn't matter how difficult it may look to you. Remember nothing is too tough for God.

   - "But I am trusting you, O Lord, saying, "You are my God" (Psalm 31:14).

   - "But when I am afraid, I will put my trust in you" (Psalm 56:3).

2. **Love From A Place That Has No Walls**

   If you really want to experience unconditional love, a love that is that ride or die love, you must first love in that same manner.

   - "Love never gives up, never loses faith, is always hopeful, and endures through every circumstance" (1 Corinthians 13:7).

   - "Always be humble and gentle. Be patient with each other, making allowance for each other's faults because of your love" (Ephesians 4:2).

3. **Forgiveness Is A Powerful Force**

   We all at one time in our life need to experience the power of forgiveness, the power of grace for something. Forgiveness can tear down walls and build the hope of possibility and above all else, it heals you.

   - "Get rid of all bitterness, rage, anger, harsh words, and slander, as well as all types of evil behavior. Instead, be kind to each other, tenderhearted, forgiving one another, just as God through Christ has forgiven you" (Ephesians 4:31-32).

4. **Seek Out Wisdom From Someone Skilled And Trusted To Help Guide You Through It**

Don't try to figure it out alone; don't become isolated and so private that you allow pride to keep you from asking for the help you need. Find someone who has a reputation for integrity and wisdom to pour into you during tough times.

- "The godly offer good counsel; they teach right from wrong" (Psalm 37:30).

- "Don't turn your back on wisdom, for she will protect you. Love her, and she will guard you. Getting wisdom is the wisest thing you can do! And whatever else you do, develop good judgment" (Proverbs 4:6-7).

5. **Pray And Don't Stop, Don't Give Up**

Prayer is the fuel that will push you from moment to moment, but it draws you closer to God and as you draw closer to Him; He will draw closer to you.

- "Never stop praying" (1 Thessalonians 5:17).

- "Come close to God and God will come close to you" (James 4:8).

Tanya Bakari

Tanya Bakari is the Director of Operations for Victory Church and holds the office of Assistant Vice President for a Fortune 500 company. Tanya is an author, speaker, and coach gifted with the ability to paint pictures with words igniting movement and change. A strategic thinker, she's led nationally recognized projects in the corporate sector.

With greater than 20 years coaching experience, Tanya has core strengths in communication and teaching leadership teams how to embrace the art of executing crucial conversations yielding positive results. Her love for coaching pushes people to achieve non-societal greatness defined only by God's standards and their personal gifts.

Tanya graduated from Liberty University acquiring a B.S. in Business Administration with an emphasis on Project Management. Tanya's working on launching a new novel titled, *All Things*; as well a book dedicated to her mother, Mae O'Neal Thomas, titled *Grieve and Grow*. Tanya leads the interest group "Girrrl Bye," which aids in thwarting debilitating thoughts telling women they aren't good enough.

Tanya has been married to the love of her life, Aalim for 22 years and they have 2 amazing sons, Aalim II and Taaj. When she's not working, she enjoys buying shoes, journaling, and reading. To reach Tanya for speaking engagements, coaching sessions, or project planning, contact her at *tanya@tanyabakari.com* or Twitter *@tnbakari*.

Chapter 2

Treasures Found In Unlikely Places

Trish DiMaggio-Zander

"For I know I have plans for you, declares the Lord, plans to prosper you and not harm you, plans to give you hope and a future." Jeremiah 29:11

From birth to death, each person in our lives is placed there purposefully by God to play a specific role. We won't always understand the reasons especially if the relationships are particularly painful. At some point however, if we open our eyes and our hearts, it will become clear. Through my story, I hope to illustrate the healing that takes place when we stand in truth, show ourselves as we are, and believe in God's power to heal us. To set some context around what I want to share with you, it's important to describe where things in this world started for me, the people around me and the role they played in my life.

My story starts with 2 parents, five older brothers, 8 older sisters and me. My parents were devout in their faith and did not believe in birth control. They left the size of their family in God's hands, and He sent fourteen of us to them. There was a large gap between me and my older siblings, except for my sister Audrey. Because of that, we have always been close. As for my other siblings, many of them didn't take so kindly to me. My parents were in their forties when I was born and by that time, they were in a much better place financially. They could offer me things that they couldn't offer my older siblings. From my perspective, this caused resentment and they viewed me as spoiled. It felt like they were determined to remind me of this often and at times in unkind ways. Although my parents tried to cushion those things as much as possible, I looked up to my older siblings; so like any child, I took to heart the things they said to me and believed them.

For many years, I thought that anything bad that happened in my life was a punishment from God. I was taught that God was powerful, but somewhere I picked up the message that if you were a good person who did good things, God rewarded you. If you were a bad person who did bad things, God punished you. Believing God was all powerful, I knew wholeheartedly He could do miraculous things; I just never believed He'd do them for me.

By the time I was in my early thirties, I wouldn't define the way I lived as good or as someone who deserved God's Love. I wasn't living at all, I was miserably existing. I was constantly searching outside of myself for something to ease the pain I felt. I used food, a new car, a new house, relationships, and alcohol. No matter how many times I turned to external things, they provided only momentary relief followed by even more devastating pain. Despite many of my own efforts, I couldn't pull my life together.

Each failed attempt at praying for God to help me get sober and ease my pain, just strengthened my belief that I was unworthy of His love. I would find out later that was the furthest thing from the truth.

The reason my prayers hadn't worked had nothing to do with being good or bad, worthy or unworthy. They didn't work because I would pray to God for help only to once again, turn around to put my faith in things and people to fix inside me; that which only God was capable of fixing. I had been convinced on such a deep level that I was undeserving of His love or help; I didn't trust He would give it to me. I did this continuously; even though I knew, none of the external things ever worked. In fact, alcohol made the situation worse and eventually, I lost everything.

Because I had placed all my faith in material possessions and people that were taken away, when they were gone, along with them went any hope I had. My close friend Donna, a minister and a person I turn to often for spiritual guidance says, "It is when all things are stripped away that we have the opportunity to see God is enough." For me to get better, it took the removal of everything in my life. All those things had been obstructing my view of the only one that could save me – God. When I began to rely upon Him for strength, things turned around. I did get sober and have stayed that way for over a decade. One day at a time with God, I rebuilt my life and that is truly a miracle because by all rights, I shouldn't even be alive to write this. Those experiences showed me the power of God's healing and would play an integral role as I would travel the sometimes tough terrain of life. That said, this is just a prelude to the story I'm about to share.

"God's will is like a jigsaw puzzle, you won't be able to see the whole picture until all the pieces are together." Danny L. Deaubé

I thought I had done the needed divine coursework through the painful experiences I had already faced; but, I would learn over and again that conscientious, continuing education and practice is required to maintain spiritual health. I did that, but I don't think my diligence was what it needed to be. May 22, 2016, marks the beginning of my next level of intense providential curriculum. It was on that day that I lost someone precious to me who I loved as my own child. My nephew, my Godson, Jovanni.

His death shattered my heart, but there were other circumstances surrounding the event that intensified my despair. It brought to the surface wounds from my childhood that I thought I had for the most part, been healed. Once again, pain would be the springboard into the healing power of God's love. Sorrow would be the lens through which I would watch God transform tragedy into triumph. Grief would become the vessel He would use to deliver His grace to me.

Jovanni and I were close, but the winter and spring before he died we became even closer. He had been staying at my house periodically. The previous August, he had a horrific experience while drinking and doing drugs with his mother and her friends. As a result, he started a recovery program. I loved having him at my house. We would sit at the island in my kitchen drinking coffee and talking about life, recovery and God. The conversations were deep and especially heartfelt. He opened up to me about things that had been troubling him; things that he said he hadn't shared with anyone.

Hearing about some of the experiences was hard. It was heartbreaking that he thought he couldn't tell anyone without being judged. He knew I understood all too well the life of active alcoholism. It's an illness that not only ravages the mind and body, it ravages the soul. It's a world of shame and secrecy where people try to maneuver through life without being found out. We learn to build walls to protect ourselves from being hurt. To hide, so that the world won't see the pathetic disgrace we believe ourselves to be. Sadly, when we barricade ourselves off to avoid hurt, we also block off the opportunity for experiencing love and connection, which are as essential to our survival as are food and water. I'll never forget that pain and loneliness.

The last time Jovanni stayed at my house, he shared with me how uncomfortable he felt at home. After he shared that with me, my husband and I had talked about having him come and live with us. The only obstacle was that he had lost his driver's license due to drinking. There wasn't public transit from our house to where he worked and we were trying to iron that out. A few days later, I texted him to see how he was doing and asked if he wanted to get together. I didn't hear back which was not like him. I texted and called him the next day with no response.

I got a bad feeling and I thought maybe he had relapsed and was feeling ashamed. I had been in recovery long enough to know that it's not effective to force people to get sober. I talked to a friend in recovery and she suggested I send one more text to let him know I was there for him when he needed to talk. I did that and I also called him and left a message telling him I was concerned about him, I loved him and there was nothing he could ever do to make me not love him nor did he have anything for which he should be ashamed. Those were the last words I ever spoke to him.

"Pain has a way of clipping our wings and keeping us from being able to fly." William Paul Young – The Shack

I remember clearly the night I learned that Jovanni died. My phone rang around 8:00 pm, I was in the bathroom washing my face. I was exhausted, so I was going to bed early. I didn't want to take the call, but a strong feeling urged me to answer. It was my sister-in-law, Darlene. She told me she was at my brother, Greg's house. She continued, saying that Jovanni was gone, and I needed go to my brother's house too. Greg is Jovanni's father and my initial thought was that they had an argument, Jovanni left, and no one could get a hold of him. I had gotten a similar message from my sister just a few weeks earlier.

When I arrived at my brother's house, I asked my sister-in-law where they thought Jovanni went. She looked at me, but said nothing. She then walked up, put her arms around me and said, "Trish, Jovanni is gone. He was killed in a car accident today." My chest got tight and my breathing shallow. I started sobbing and asked her what happened? My oldest brother Joey stepped in, gave me a hug and told me our brother needed us now and that we had to be strong for him. I tried to pull it together as much as possible and I walked into the house and went up and gave Greg a hug. I asked him what happened and he said he didn't know all the details, just that Jovanni was with his friend Cory and they were in a car accident.

The rest of the night was a bit crazy. Soon, my brother's house was full of friends and family and I started to get overwhelmed. Multiple conversations were taking place at once with people talking over each other. I started feeling like I was invisible and getting lost in the sea of chaos, in which I grew up. I was anxiety ridden and I decided I needed to go home. When I got there, my husband was waiting up for me. He gave me a hug and asked me what happened? I told him the little that I knew which basically was that Jovanni was killed in a car accident. Everything felt surreal.

As Jovanni's aunt, more importantly his godmother, I expressed very clearly that I wanted to be involved in the planning of his funeral. It was important to and for me to help make his service beautiful. Being a writer, I especially wanted to help with his obituary. My brother was distraught so several of my sisters were helping to put together funeral arrangements. They promised me I would be included.

The Monday evening before Jovanni's funeral, I went to my brother, Greg's house. After everyone cleared out, I had a conversation with just him. We had never really talked like that before, so it meant a lot to me. We reminisced about Jovanni's life both the good and the challenges. My brother and Jovanni's mother, Brenda, had gone through a bitter divorce several years earlier. There were many things that contributed to it, but primarily it was her drinking. My brother loved and I believe still does love her. However, even though his love for her didn't stop, he knew her drinking was destructive; not only to her, but those around her. Knowing the state she was in, he knew that she was not healthy for Jovanni, especially while he was trying to stay sober. Both he and one of my sisters, cautioned him about that. There had already been multiple instances where she encouraged him to drink with her. Those situations left Jovanni emotionally and physically devastated. The incident the August before landed him in the hospital.

By late morning the next day, I hadn't heard from my sisters who were working on the funeral arrangements. I sent a text message and didn't get a response. I decided to put together a video of pictures for the memorial. Finally, in the afternoon about 1:30, I called again and got a hold of them. I asked when they were going to go pick out flowers and go to the funeral home. I was told that they had already done that along with writing and submitting the obituary. My sister said, they forgot to call me. I was devastated that I hadn't been included. When I read the obituary for my beautiful, vibrant Godson, it felt cold and emotionless to me and I was crushed. It didn't illustrate the richness of Jovanni's life or who he was.It merely reported facts. He deserved better than that.

To add insult to injury, my sisters who organized Jovanni's funeral wrote a few thoughts about him and what he meant to them. Jovanni's godfather was invited to do the same. The priest was asked to share the thoughts at the service. Even though I shared multiple times how much it meant to me to be to be involved, I was excluded from that as well. After the service, my sister-in-law Darlene could see how hurt I was and she came up and hugged me. I couldn't stay for the reception after because I was so upset and couldn't stop crying. At home, my husband did what he could to try and comfort me.

At that point, I couldn't talk nor did I want to; but I did text my sisters to tell them how I felt. Later, one of them called me from my brother's house. I could hear people in the background. When she started talking, it felt like everything she said dismissed my feelings. She also told me that people thought I was being dramatic. I found out later that they had special candles made and that only specific people in my family received them, I was never offered one. The things they did just kept cutting deeper and deeper. I thought surely, all those things could not have been a coincidence and I thought they were cruel. Wasn't it enough that I was in pain from my nephew's death? Those old horrible feelings from my childhood rose to the surface. I felt rejected, unloved and like an outsider inside my own family. I thought that by now as adults, most of this stuff had been worked through. I wondered how they could still hold so much resentment for me. I was convinced they hated me. My hurt quickly turned into anger. How dare they say I was being dramatic!

Therefore, I tell you, all that you ask for in prayer, believe that you will receive it and it shall be yours. (Mark 11:24)

I decided to call a friend who is a priest. I shared everything with him and asked him if I was being dramatic in how I felt. He told me, "No," I wasn't being dramatic at all. He explained that funeral services are a sacred rite of passage. They are a call to reflect even more deeply on our spiritual beliefs about life and death. They are a way to help with the grief process and for families and friends to come together for love and support. He said as Jovanni's aunt but especially as his godmother, it would be expected that I be involved. He put into words all I had been feeling. It felt good that someone understood how important it was that I participate in returning to God the precious gift He so lovingly bestowed upon my life. Even if it was just for a short time. I shared how angry I was about it all and he told me it was okay to have those emotions, but eventually I would have to resolve them if I wanted to get through all this. He told me I should pray for my family and for God to help me see things differently.

I also talked to friends in recovery who immediately told me the same thing and they added that I needed to be specific, as I prayed for my family's happiness and healing. They reminded me I could not afford to stay angry, whether seemingly justified or not. That was poison for my soul and my recovery. My sister Jeanie, who has also been a loving support, told me to pray and ask God to help me with forgiveness. In my grief, I didn't think they deserved my prayers. One of my friends suggested I still do it. She even told me I could start out by telling God I was praying for them even though I didn't mean it, He knew anyway. The next thing she said was key and that was to ask God for the willingness to be willing for my heart to change. It was the best I could do in the moment.

The following months felt unbearable. I felt like I had failed Jovanni and every night as I said my prayers, I would talk to him. I apologized to him continually for not being there for him more. As I grieved for him, I was still angry at my family. I kept praying even though I didn't feel like it was working. Then another tragedy struck. The loss of my brother Joey, to suicide. I wasn't ready for another loss (but that is a story for another time). The day of my brother's funeral, I was naturally sad. It was also bringing up everything I felt at Jovanni's funeral. I walked in the church and out of the corner of my eye, I noticed Jovanni's mother. She was one person for whom I had held deep contempt and it became stronger after Jovanni's death. I thought, "God, please don't let her come up to me." As she started walking towards me, I thought, "God, please help me be nice." She said, "Hello," and I could smell alcohol on her breath. I thought, how disrespectful she was for coming to my brother's funeral in that condition.

We exchanged a few words and suddenly, a feeling of peace came over me. The hatred I felt was gone and replaced with compassion. Instead, I now saw a person who was doing the best they could in that moment under very difficult circumstances. I saw clearly that she already carried a heavy burden within her and she did not need me to add to it. Then I thought of the people in my family I had been so mad at and the feelings of anger toward them lifted too. Any ill thoughts I had, left. I hadn't felt peace like that in a long time. Later that day, my friend Becky called. I told her what happened and she said, "Trish, that was the grace of God."

"Look at a stone cutter hammering away at his rock perhaps a hundred times without as much as a crack showing in it. Yet at the hundred-and-first blow it will split in two and I know it was not the last blow that did it, but all that had gone before." Jacob Riis

Whenever I hear this quote, it reminds me of how often and long I prayed to God to end my pain before finding sobriety. It sometimes felt like He wasn't listening but in the end, He delivered me from that hell. It reminds me that I need to stay in constant contact with God during the good times, but especially during painful times. When I keep moving forward in faith, He is working miracles on my behalf; whether I see them or not. As I am writing this, the stone cutter quote also makes me think of diamonds; one of the most precious jewels that exists. Diamonds are hidden in what appears at first to be ugly worthless rocks. The rock must be broken open, cut and polished to reveal its brilliance. The utmost care and mastery are required when doing this, it is not immediate. I think with God, it's the same. He always sees everyone's brilliance, even when we do not and He is constantly working on us all.

Through Jovanni's life, I learned a great deal about love and through his death I learned in a deeper and more profound way about the power of love. Those lessons were seared into my heart and will stay there. When he comes to mind, I think about how much he loved his family and friends no matter what their faults were; which is probably why people were drawn to him. Like God, he could see beyond the external. He had his struggles as we all do, in our humanness. Yet, in the face of that, he always returned to love. He was and is an example of the kind of person I think God wants everyone to be. Even when we are hurt, even when we think people don't love us.

I have learned that my family loves me in the way they are capable of loving me. When we feel hurt because people don't accept or love us, feeling whole doesn't occur when they finally do. Healing takes place when I offer to them the same love and acceptance I want from them. It is in those moments that I experience the true love of God. He forces no one to love Him and neither should we. I no longer believe God causes me pain or bad things to happen in my life to punish me. God is pure love and pure love never harms. I believe it is in our humanness that we wound each other in word or deed. I believe that it is life itself that brings us difficulties. The role God plays is one of Divine Physician; who in those times, wants me to bring my sorrow and pain to Him so He can mend the wounds I carry. The only requirement is I must be willing to let Him in to heal me. I fought that for a long time. All of the above experiences have helped me to realize that I can now stop and ask God to help me to see through His eyes when I see what might appear to be an ugly rock in my path. It may not happen immediately, but eventually, that ugly rock turns into a precious jewel.

The difficulties in my life are what brought me closer to my Creator. I am reminded that with Him, treasures are found in the most unlikely places. The five treasures (lessons learned) that continue to resonate with me as a result of the experiences I shared above are:

1. The largest blessings in my life have often been disguised as agonizing experiences.

2. I have to show myself completely to God in order to be healed. Not because God doesn't already see the places within me that need healing; but because often, it is I who doesn't see the places within me that need healing.

3. Pain can sometimes obstruct my view and make me feel as though God has abandoned me. In fact, that is when He is closest to me. Over again in the Bible, we see that Jesus went wherever there was someone in pain.

4. God will always heal that pain *if* I am willing to receive His healing.

5. In the words of my father — "Life without God is purpose without meaning."

Trish DiMaggio-Zander

Trish DiMaggio-Zander is a writer, blogger, and strategic leader who has professional career experience in lending, sales, and marketing. She is a woman with both purpose and passion which she uses as a platform to assist others in finding their strength in the midst of adversity. Trish is a featured columnist on the blog reneweveryday. com where her articles not only captivate, but are meant to motivate, encourage, and positively impact the lives of her audience.

Trish graduated summa cum laude from Ashford University earning a Bachelor's Degree in Psychology. Deemed a champion for change, Trish uses her educational, professional, and personal experience as a conduit in which to bring real life issues for recovery and redemption to the surface to create an environment for open dialogue and life altering discussions. Trish is a woman of God who serves at and is a member of St. John The Baptist Catholic Church in Waunakee, WI. Trish is married to her husband and partner for life, Doug and they are the proud parents of 2 fur babies, Cleo and Sophie.

To connect with Trish for speaking engagements and other partnership opportunities, email her at *trish.dimaggiozander@gmail.com.*

Chapter 3

Season of the Wait
Angela Clay

"Do not be anxious about anything, but in every situation, by prayer and petition, with thanksgiving, present your requests to God. And the peace of God, which transcends all understanding, will guard your hearts and your minds in Christ Jesus." Philippians 4:6-7

Oh my God! This brother was 6'2, dark skin, muscular and clean-cut with a bald head. He had structurally defined facial features, the kind you would see modeling in a GQ magazine. I thought to myself, "I really don't like his attire. Those wrangler jeans and t-shirt got to go! But that's an easy fix." His physique and chocolate skin had me shook. I had always dreamed of a guy artistically molded just like him. He even resonated in my prayers. Come through Jesus!

Talk about praying! It's ironic that I met him at church. We would cross paths randomly at church and he would greet me with an inviting, "Hello," and consistently compliment how well-mannered and polite my daughter,

Tink was. I would smile courteously and continue on my way home for my Sunday nap. This experience would repeat itself for months. One day, a guy friend of mine came over excited and exclaimed, "Angie, I have the perfect guy for you!" He shared that the fellow was financially stable, lived in his own place, attends church regularly and had no kids. I responded, "He sounds like a perfect catch! What's wrong with him?" He replied, "He's a great guy. He just needs a sophisticated lady in his life." "What the heck? I'll give it a try," I said.

My number was given to the "perfect guy." An hour later, I received a call. Who would have known that it was the very same "Chocolate Drop" I had been crushing on? My friends even referred to him by that moniker because I would go on and on about my infatuation over this handsome guy from church. During our first conversation, we talked for hours and hours. We discussed dating with a purpose and how neither one of us were particularly looking for a relationship. He seemed to comfortably come back to the heartbreak from his previous relationship that had concluded six months prior. Some of the things that stuck out was that it was an interracial relationship. I could tell from the dialogue that he really admired this woman. She was beautiful, smart, and athletic; but she left him feeling unappreciated and emasculated. This woman had an impact on him that would haunt him emotionally for a while. I provided comfort and expressed that I would date him until his heart healed.

For 11 months, we enjoyed being in each other's space with no commitment and zero pressure. We connected, vibed, and developed a genuine friendship. Because we committed to date with a purpose, we attended events together; went to Bible study and church, and even started "family date nights," with my daughter. He would open car doors, check in with me throughout the day, and ask me if I needed anything. I had never dated anyone like this and the thing that I loved most about him was that he loved my daughter. I had prayed countless nights for my Boaz. "Rejoice in the Lord always. I will say it again rejoice" (Philippians 4:4). My life seemed to finally come together. I thought, "God had done it!" He was truly the love of my life.

The Good

Our bond strengthened and we became a staple to our family and friends. We could no longer contain this beautiful thing we had found and we wanted to scream from the mountain tops that we both found our perfect match. Somehow, the love we exuded began to impact the lives of those we were connected to. Strangers would even compliment us. Everyone was so happy because we were so happy and they had faith that our love could stand tests, flourish, and soar. The courtship was exhilarating. We would even try to one up each other on ideas for date night.

One beautiful memory I have is, I planned a scavenger hunt, boat ride with an intimate picnic, complete with a Frankie Beverly and Maze concert on his birthday. He was astonished at the effort and time that was involved in planning something especially for him, since he had never experienced this before. Chocolate Drop took Tink on plenty of date nights as well, including Six Flags, water parks, tent movie nights, and surprise lunch dates. The moment that stands out most, was the Father-Daughter dance. They were both so cute in their 60's get up, and my heart was overwhelmed with joy. When they returned home from the dance, Tink excitedly said, "Momma we had so much fun, but he was embarrassing me on the dance floor!" Chocolate Drop responded with, "I was killing the other dads with the Nae-Nae!"

I saw him as the "perfect man." He was gentle, loving, patient, affectionate, and fathering. They would mow the lawn, wash and put gas in the car; he also taught her how to ride her motorcycle, wash the dishes, and learn how to count money. He would rush to pick her up from school; hold her hand as he protected her on the street. He would even attend practices and cheer with my baby. He was a damn good father figure. She would often say, "He's going to be my dad when you guys get married!"

We attended the Church's gala for a family date night; my daughter was a beautiful princess, I had my king, and I was the queen. We two-stepped the entire night, just us three. People admired our relationship as we portrayed the image of a true, loving family. They would say we were the prototype of love and hope and I believed it too.

The Bad

As expected in any relationship, every day is not going to be sunshine and roses. The concerns soon began to rise above the water. While we were comfortably enjoying my family holidays, birthdays, family night out, Sunday dinners, I never seemed to be invited to be with his family. This began to bother me and I developed feelings of inadequacy, doubts of his dedication, and shame. I became resentful. He often said, "My family isn't like your family." I was confused, but I somehow knew what he was referring to. His family was multi-cultural and educated and my family would be deemed as more urban, uncultured, uneducated and perceived as ghetto. I would ask him about what he thought about that. I believed there was a learning opportunity for him to explore and challenge his perceptions. I informed him about the diversity of my family, my job, and sent him educational sites to inform him about my experience with cultural diversity. We discussed being comfortable in your own skin. He shared that he had always felt ostracized, whereas other nationalities seemed to embrace him. He was teased as a child because of his dark skin, and he shared that it took time to get to the point where he could embrace his dark skin. This now made sense to me as I would always question why a man who seemed to have so much in his favor desired to date outside of his race.

As a single black mother, I took pride in my accomplishments. He respected that I was educated, career- oriented, independent, and successful; however these achievements caused insecurities within him. He expressed feelings of inferiority and I felt confused because I felt he was sufficient. I could not be proud of myself because this made him feel insecure.

Another area of test was the area of finance. We both come from poverty-stricken childhoods, but we had *completely* different views on how we spent money. He patterned his spending after Dave Ramsey (save) and I believed in mindfully enjoying the fruits of my labor. While the relationship was ideal in most aspects, around the 3-year mark, I began to feel as if we were still dating with a purpose. I recalled a conversation we had earlier in our relationship, where I expressed that I did not desire to date for years, but expected to marry and be an example to Tink. I remember feeling that this conversation made him uncomfortable, leading me to question if marriage was a desire for our future together. I saw signs of indecisiveness and I grew resentful and decided that I no longer wanted to be intimate with someone that was unsure about our future. This was an emotional rollercoaster for both of us; as we seemed to be on two separate pages. I began to detach and channel my energy into my spirituality and the possibility of being single once again.

The relationship was on unstable ground; but in effort to save us, we began pre-marital counseling. Two sessions in, our relationship went cold. He showed disinterest in the reading material, completing assignments, and actively participating in therapy. I could tell something was wrong; I knew we were in trouble. Our communication dwindled. I felt lonely and confused and I sought after God and asked Him to reveal and make clear the purpose of our relationship. We talked and he eventually revealed that there had been several acts of infidelity. I was crushed. I remember being disgusted as he cried and pleaded on bended knee. I was quiet and numb to the revelation he had revealed. When we were interrupted by my daughter stating she was hungry, I took this as my chance to ask him to leave. After several failed requests, he continued to cry hysterically on my bathroom floor. I was completely numb, calm voice, no tears, no reaction. I called a mutual friend to come get him before I'd kill him and our friend convinced him to leave. As he left, Tink came running with excitement to the top step, calling out to him. He never turned back. With a whimpering, quiet voice he said, "I have to go. I'll see you later."

The break up was pretty rough. Not many people were aware that we were taking time apart. Tink would inquire why he had not been over, while I tried to reinsert myself back into the singles game and reestablish my independence. Tink was my focal point. Being a mother was most important. At the end of the day, I was left with anger and wonder. I was on a spiritual journey and I would ask God if my relationship was reconcilable. I was grounded by my faith, staying active in church, and imparting into my daughter's life. I would still see him on

Sundays and my stomach would be in knots as Tink would run up to him with open arms. I was torn because I did not want to see him, talk to him, or be around this guy that broke my heart into pieces.It was obvious that we were separated as others took note of our distance. Because I was uncomfortable with the things that took place in our relationship, I bottled up the fact that we were apart. I was embarrassed, ashamed, and hurt. Tink took it harder than I did. Her world was shaken and she was confused, lost, and wounded.

I began processing my situation with friends and they attempted to keep me encouraged; but felt the situation was foul. However, they were still team Chocolate Drop. They wanted to see us win. He would inquire with one of my best friends on the status of our relationship and she would encourage him to fight for it and express his love. So many nights, I would get on my knees and pray because I wanted to forgive him. I did not want to be angry, so I smiled every day, but I remained in constant prayer. "Present your requests to God and the peace of God which transcends all understanding" (Philippians 4:6). God was really working on my heart as I was often led to call him. Contradictory of what I wanted to do, God kept giving me this overwhelming feeling to reach out to him to get things resolved. Just like that, after a tearful conversation, we committed to giving it one more shot.

With remorse and a promise to fully commit, we were on a journey for love. He executed a plan and discussed the steps to a thriving, successful companionship. With several concerns about trust, I expressed that if this was his desire, there would have to be change and a long-term goal of a life-long marriage. I definitely could not take any more games and bullshit from Chocolate Drop. While others seemed to move forward with life and have successful relationships,

I was taken back by the disappointment that had taken place with us. Discussed in detail, my expectations were minimal. I expressed my needs and waited to observe his actions. My close friend encouraged me to be patient, I had no idea that she and Chocolate Drop were ring shopping. I did recall several conversations with her about rings, engagements, and things of the sort.

July 3, 2015, I went out with friends and while relaxing at a poolside bar, I wondered if he was out being unfaithful. Later in the day, he texted and he requested that I come over. I had felt disconnected from him earlier, so I reluctantly said yes. When I arrived, we both in our feelings and we cuddled in the quiet. Comfortable and tired from the day, I fell asleep. At approximately 3:30am, while we transitioned from the couch to the bed, he remained in the restroom for what seemed like forever. I tried not be annoyed by the light that kept me from falling asleep. For a moment, I opened my eyes and there he was before me on bended knee! I was sleepy and confused. As he stuttered shakily with tears in his eyes and grinned through his speech, reality set in that he was proposing to me. He cracked open the ring box and said, "One thing is sure. I cannot live without you and Tink." I had been waiting for this day for three years and that day I said, "YES," to the love of my life. The 4th of July would never be same. The season of the wait was over.

As excitement filled our lives, we both shared the good news with our loved ones and friends and we began wedding planning. We looked at venues, tasted food and wine, and planned for the perfect wedding. Tink was very prominent in the process and she helped me find the perfect wedding dress. She exclaimed that I was a princess and I should look beautiful, just like Cinderella. My dress was regal with hand-stitched beading, a large train, and a sexy low v-cut bodice. We were full of excitement and joy. Chocolate Drop set the wedding date for September 4, 2016, and we planned everything for our special day. With so many people invested into our love journey, we decided on two engagement celebrations. Family and friends joined us for drinks on the rooftop in downtown Dallas and for the second celebration, we took an exquisite boat ride on Rockwall Lake. With a Great Gatsby wedding theme, deposits were paid for the venue, DJ, and photographer, as well as for additional items, totaling over $5000.

Premarital counseling was gut-wrenching, as we set out to finish the process. Fear of failing to complete it brought anxiety; however, we were thriving and both seemed committed. We learned so many things about each other, our relationship, and acquired skills that would be conducive to marital success. In the late fall, we successfully completed counseling and I was hopeful for our future as 2016 quickly approached. I was in a beautiful space. I attended New Year's Eve service and my heart was filled with joy and anticipation of the great things to come. I turned to him at the stroke of midnight and said, "2015 has been a rough year, but I am looking forward to being your wife." He addressed me as, "Mrs. Chocolate Drop," and exclaimed how beautiful that name sounded.

The Ugly

While I was on cloud 9, I began to feel a shift with us. I wasn't sure where this energy came from because we were still working towards our goals. I noticed that his excitement dwindled as we discussed every facet of life, except the wedding. I observed that there seemed to be reservations, and he became distant. He started to express concerns of doubt, "What if we don't work out? How will we split our assets? What if I am not a good husband?"

He began to vocalize goals that he had yet to attain for himself and expressed how I independently acquired things that he had not contributed to. I found it ironic that we attended church Sunday after Sunday, participated in Bible Study, and prayed together, yet he had not grown stronger in his faith. These discussions created anxiety for me, but I wanted to keep him encouraged and strong. I attributed these doubts and fears to him having cold feet. I would often express that I, myself was scared shitless. I explained that we were both entering new territory and would both be giving up our lives as single individuals. This was a big deal to us both, as I have never lived with a man, shared finances, nor had another disciplinarian for my child. This would definitely be an adjustment for me too. I assured him that he was not alone. With communication and honesty these fears seemed to relinquish for the moment.

Ultimately, the behaviors, thoughts, and insecurities never subsided as they would appear in our future conversations. With countless dialogue concerning these topics, doubts that he could carry our household came to surface. I often wondered if he would flee when times turned tough or how he would deal with life's challenges. I remember like it was yesterday. It was a gloomy day in late January. I went to his job to check-in after several failed calls. He came down with a concerned look in his eyes. As we walked along downtown Fort Worth, the energy was dry, so I asked, "What is wrong with you?" I wasn't expecting to hear him say, "I don't want to get married." My stomach dropped to the pavement in disbelief. I was thinking, "Not again!" My follow-up question: "You don't want to be married or you don't want to marry me?" He replied "I don't want to get married right now." I questioned what he meant 'right now'; as the wedding was just seven months away. Although I was distraught by what was taking place, I wanted to hear him out. We proceeded to walk towards the car, both quiet with our thoughts in tow. It felt like hours of sitting there discussing where these emotions where coming from and where we would go from here. It was purposeful for me to remain gentle with my responses and present understanding and compassion. I did not want to shun him for expressing his truth, but I needed to process and simply think. When he left the car, I recall sitting in the car overwhelmed with emotion. How did we get here, yet again? Hours felt like days and days felt like weeks as our communication dwindled. The conversation replayed over and over in my head like lyrics to a song that you cannot forget. I grew angry and resentful. I thought, "How dare you not want to marry me? The nerve of you!"

While I was not perfect, I felt perfect for him. I grew him, made him better, and provided purpose to his existence. As several close family and friends were aware of our dilemma, I knew I would have to explain to the world how the marriage they rooted for and prayed for was not happening. People wanted to know how this could happen, they wanted to know the details, often asking: "How did this happen? What do you mean the wedding is off? Do you think it's just cold feet?" I didn't know how to answer these questions, but I knew that I did not want to keep having this conversation. I decided to make a public statement regarding it on Facebook. It was important to remain kind when I expressed that it was a mutual decision to call off the wedding. I thanked everyone for their support and for having gone on this love journey with us.

People were enraged, and commented, "What in hell?" They were dismayed and let down. Several personal messages were sent questioning his integrity, character, and faith. Some wondered how he could mess up, come into my and my daughter's life and run out on us. Comments that I should remove the social media post and not let the devil have the joy were expressed, and many responded with hope and prayers that we would reconcile and continue towards marriage. I was in despair, but I did not want people to bash this man that I loved so dearly.

After several weeks of sadness and depression, days of prying myself out of bed just to feed my daughter and taking a leave of absence from my job for emotional distress, I realized I had to persevere. Not for me, but for my daughter. I questioned God about my experiences, not just with the present situation, but my entire life. I questioned what purpose he had for me and the reason for this big heartbreak. I felt alone and wondered where my friends were during this dark time. It seemed as if after a week of check-ins they felt I was okay, but I wasn't, I was an emotional wreck.

I started counseling and was prescribed anxiety and sleep medications. More insecurities developed and I wondered if I was good enough. Thoughts of regret and the wonder of what I could have done to make things different pervaded my thoughts. Not only was I affected, Tink regressed in her academics and questioned why Chocolate Drop did not want to be her dad. She did not understand why we were not going to be a family because we didn't argue. She reached out with calls and texts to him, but he did not respond. I was furious that he would do this to her after being the most prominent father figure in life. The reality set in that this relationship was over because I could not go back after he intentionally abandoned my daughter. I wanted to wake up from this nightmare. I just wanted to be free from this hold. I just wanted to move on with my life. I leaped into my faith to see me through. I asked God to give me peace and forgiveness and I focused on me, my family, health, career, and faith. Each day, my walk seemed a little lighter.

Today, I still have hopes for marriage; although I am not aware of what God's plan is for me. At times, I still struggle with the acceptance of being single and I am still in the season of the wait. God transformed my heart and instilled forgiveness and today Chocolate Drop fosters the relationship with my daughter and we are in an amicable space.

Moments of Reflection

Even when you are in your darkest place and may not understand what God is doing in your life, the word enlightens us to be anxious for nothing, but pray about all things. There is a lesson in every experience and I reflect on scriptures from Philippians.

"Do not be anxious about anything, but in every situation, by prayer and petition, with thanksgiving, present your requests to God. And the peace of God, which transcends all understanding, will guard your hearts and your minds in Christ Jesus." (Philippians 4:6-7)

"Whatever you have learned or received or heard from me or seen in me- put it to practice and the God of peace will be with you." (Philippians 4:9)

"I am not saying this because I am in need, for I have learned to be content whatever the circumstances. I know what it is to be in need, and I know what it is to have plenty. I have learned the secret of being content in any and every situation, whether well fed or hungry, whether living in plenty or in want. I can do all this through him who gives me strength." (Philippians 4:11-13)

Five Lessons Learned Throughout My Experience:

1. I am not a victim; I am victorious. Although I desire marriage, it's my waiting season. God said not yet. Although I don't understand, I have to remember, He knows the desires of my heart.

2. Let go, forgive, and push through. When I was at, what seemed like, the darkest place in my life, God saw fit for me to forgive; even when people didn't understand how or why.

3. I often question why God keeps choosing me? But why not me? Every test He's given me, there has not been a situation where there wasn't a testimony; where I could look back and think only God could see me through that experience.

4. Peace be still. Even in my singleness, as hard as it may be at times, I've asked God if He doesn't see marriage in my future, to allow me to be at peace and content with whatever plans He has for my life.

5. Count it all joy! I don't look like what I've been through because it's all a part of love, life and lessons learned.

Angela Clay

Angela Clay is a Director of Social Services who has dedicated her professional career to the social services arena targeting the needs of men, women, and children who have been impacted by homelessness, domestic violence, and sexual predatory behavior. Deemed a strategic leader, her skilled competencies coupled with her heart to both give and serve has prompted her to earn multiple awards which recognize her accomplishments to both educate and empower victims through emotional support.

Angela earned her Master of Social Work Degree from The University of Texas @ Arlington, Arlington, Texas after having earned a Bachelor of Social Work Degree from Tarleton State University, Stephenville, Texas. A member of Zeta Phi Beta Sorority Incorporated, Angela uses both her career accomplishments and educational experience to champion for both social awareness and support of the underserved within the Dallas Fort Worth Metroplex.

Along with being an amazing mother to her beautiful daughter, Amaris {Tink}, Angela serves in the choir and is under the leadership of Dr. Douglas E. Brown of Great Commission Baptist Church, Fort Worth Texas. In her spare time, Angela enjoys singing, traveling, and above all, spending quality time with Amaris and their pet Pomeranian, "Chevy Love."

Connect with Angela for speaking engagements, workshops, and conferences @ *msaclay99@gmail.com.*

Chapter 4

The Journey of Believing
Ashley Dudley

"I believe; help my unbelief." Mark 9:24

From birth until death, we are all on a journey and throughout it, we will not know all the time where we are going. I am a firm believer in defining your path and your own journey; but to always remember the Creator of the journey. He will always place us where we need to go.

"Faith is the substance of things hoped for, the evidence of things not seen." Hebrews 11:1

I researched to understand if there is a difference between faith and believing. Reverend Rene Brown states that the *Nelson Bible Dictionary* defines faith as a belief in or confident attitude toward God, involving commitment to his will for one's life. Nelson also says that belief is to place one's trust in God's truth.

Many times on the journey, we want results to happen instantly and miraculously. Unfortunately, it just does not happen that way; and if it does, it was supposed to. I remember this line from a gospel song that says, "For the race isn't given to the swift nor to the strong, but the one who endures till the end." We will be able to complete some things quickly on our journey, while other things will take time. I am going to share a portion of my journey with you and the lessons learned along the way. My journey has its share of ups and downs; along with the joys and pains. However, I can truly say that I am thankful for where I've been, where I am and where I am going.

The beginning of my journey goes back to 2009 when I first got my apartment. I had graduated from Texas Woman's University the previous year and was getting accustomed to being on my own and enjoying work. My place was not decked out or fully furnished; but as time went along, I got what I needed. In the last quarter of the year, my focus was to begin working towards a master's degree. This was a goal I desired to see come to fruition because I knew how much my career would stem from this.

When starting out on a new journey, you may think you need to keep up with the Joneses' or have all the material things. You may think you need every contact and connection you have made through life too. Sometimes, you just need the necessities and the important people in your circle. Going along the journey, you can add to what you have, along the way. If you have too much or too many people around you starting out, it may weigh you down and cause you to lose focus.

My mind was set on attending Dallas Theological Seminary to earn a degree in Biblical Counseling. I began to prepare to complete the application and submitting the requirements that were asked for. Fast forward to February 2010, I found out that I was pregnant. Knowing that this didn't mean that my life was over, I still could not BELIEVE I was pregnant. I admit that I was scared and knew that some readjustments would be made in my life, which was my biggest concern. However, I was excited because I would be bringing life into the world. As I now look back to this particular time, I often wonder if I had missed out on living a single life before becoming a parent? I know this was a mistake, but there are no regrets because my daughter is a definite blessing in my life. I asked the Lord for forgiveness because, at this time, I felt that I needed Him more than ever before. Even though His forgiveness gave me a sense of peace, I was still ashamed of being pregnant.

I told my parents within a couple of weeks after finding out and although they were stunned, they gave me support along the way. Over time, it became easier to discuss my pregnancy and prepare for my daughter with my parents. I acknowledged God's grace and mercy throughout the pregnancy because it was only Him that carried me through. I had a desire to be more active and help others, but the pregnancy caused a shift with those things. I had been selected at my church to be a facilitator to disciple teen girls and I would now have to sit down from fulfilling that role, and I was okay with that. It was advised that I focus on my pregnancy and becoming a mother, but later it could be revisited if I was still interested. My desire to start on my master's degree would have to be placed on hold for a while too.

The journey of life may have detours which may cause delays. We must remember that these delays are not denials. Some of you may have heard that God has three answers: yes, no and wait. I have come to learn that His no's and waits are just as good and sometimes even better than His yes'.

I did not come out and tell family and friends quickly, but in time as they found out, they were happy and supportive. I recall a co-worker messaging me on Facebook, wanting to share something that another co-worker said about me. While I was curious, I did not ask what was said. I told myself at that moment that God has the final say. It didn't matter what people thought about me or said. What God said, is all that mattered.

Thank God for His support and those who walk faithfully with you on your journey. Sometimes you need a push, encouragement, and support; and while the journey is your own, you cannot always survive alone.

From the time I found out I was pregnant, I began preparing for life with a little one. By May, I found out that I would be giving birth to my daughter. I also began seeking out and applying for jobs. With what I was making, I would need more income to provide for my daughter and me. I am not ashamed to say that I applied for Medicaid and WIC and received it. Both programs were a true blessing for me at that time. On my due date, October 20, guess where I was at… work! I remember being recognized at the team meeting that day for work. I worked right up to the weekend and took off. The following week, I gave birth to the most beautiful girl after carrying her for 40 weeks and 6 days!

So, life began as a single parent. I enjoyed being off six weeks, but I was still looking and applying for jobs and also thinking ahead for our lives. In mid-November, I received a notice that my application had been reviewed for a job as a Nutritionist. In December, the job asked for me to come in and take a test and on the following day, I was interviewed. The following three weeks as I waited to hear from that job, I was not scheduled to work on Sundays at my current job. I was very happy because it allowed me to spend time with my daughter and I could also attend church. I also felt that I would not be at this job too much longer. One day, I received a call from someone in Human Resources who wanted to verify my references. It was the next day or so that I received another call and I was offered the position. I accepted the position and in January 2011, I was now a nutritionist! Once I saw the salary in my welcome letter, I was amazed and thankful for the provision. I knew that I would be able to give God what was due to Him and provide for my home. While I had been grateful to have worked at a hospital in my field, I was even more thankful that I now had the opportunity to fully put my degree to work.

So, my journey continued as I was now working a true full-time job with benefits and was a single parent. Thinking back during my daughter's first year of life, it went by so quickly. I recall doing my best to capture the moments of my daughter while doing my best to enjoy life. Trying to manage everything by yourself is not easy.

In the journey of new beginnings, it can be overwhelming in a positive or negative way. New beginnings are exciting because it is something different, yet it can be challenging at the same time; as your routine or your way of doing things may have to change. The question is, will you truly embrace your new beginning? If a new beginning starts off negative, will you change your outlook, or will it stay the same? Will you make the necessary changes for it to become positive?

During the summer of 2011, my mind was still set on attending graduate school to pursue counseling. I knew taking online courses would be best, so I began to do my research. I did some studying for the GRE, but I did not want to take the test (just keeping it real). I discovered Liberty University and knew this had to be the school. They are a Christian school, but I liked how they included a secular outlook which helped expand my worldview approach. I remember contacting the school to see what was required for their admission process and got everything together. It turned out that I didn't have to take the GRE! That June, I was accepted into their Master of Arts in Human Services program. I was excited to begin the program because I knew that nothing and no one could stop me.

Determination is needed for the journey. Do not lose sight of your goals. Sometimes, you may have to take a few steps back but pick back up where you left off. Keep pushing forward.

In October, my daughter turned one and I began taking courses. I enjoyed the classes, but I was having to learn how to balance family, school, and work. I will not forget that December having to write two papers which were ten pages or more. I completed both papers past the deadline, but I received a passing grade. As I juggled all of this, there were a few times I had taken a postpartum depression quiz. While not rating high for depression, I still felt at times like I was hopeless and alone. Although I was very happy about being the parent of a beautiful baby girl, attending graduate school, and having my new job, something just did not feel right.

One day, I talked to a friend about how I was feeling. She asked if I ever take out time for myself or do anything fun? Yes, I was doing those things; but it still was not enough. I finally went to the doctor at the beginning of 2012 and was diagnosed with minor depression. I was put on medication and could begin to see a difference within a few weeks. I felt a lot better and my mind seemed clearer. A follow-up with the doctor was scheduled after being on the medication for three months. She prescribed the medication for another three months and suggested another follow-up. One day in June, I decided to slowly take myself off the medication. There was no follow-up scheduled with my doctor, but I recall just feeling better. I remember telling God that I trusted Him as I got off the medication.

Please seek counsel from your doctor if you are wanting to get off of any current medication(s) for mental or medical reasons. It is always best to know from your doctor so you will not be in danger as well as prevent any type of side effects.

Let me put this disclaimer out there: while I am not a licensed professional counselor yet, if you believe you need to seek mental health treatment, please seek it. The doctor had recommended counseling, but I did not do it. I felt I would not have time, however, the medication did work. There is nothing wrong with talking out your problems and there is nothing wrong with medication. The main importance is finding the counselor who best suits you and addressing your concerns. If medication is needed; it is important to take the right one and knowing when you need to no longer take it, or if you will need to continue it.

Besides dealing with the depression, 2012 was turning out to be a pretty good year. After I completed the spring semester, I began to contemplate studying counseling. A Human Services degree would not get me exactly where I desired to be. I had considered school counseling, thinking I would like the school setting, but I had also considered becoming a reading specialist.

So, it was back to the drawing board to review schools and their programs. I really enjoyed Liberty, but they were not offering their complete counseling program online. Because of this, I enrolled in the school counseling program and was accepted. Fortunately for me, the online counseling program became available 100% online, so I quickly applied and was accepted. I was happy because I knew that this was what I wanted my career to be.

Going down the journey of life, you may have a clear vision of where you want to go. You can get sidetracked by people, things or situations. Trying something new or different may be of interest to you and there is nothing wrong with that; just don't take the easy way out. Sometimes we can choose to go a different route only to discover the first route was the best route. Do not waste time staying on a different route if you know where you are supposed to be headed.

In the Spring of 2013, I began my classes and I was enjoying it. Life was still going well as I was rolling with the punches. I will never forget in June of that year, I attended a women's event that my friend invited me to. I was excited about attending and my spirit was full of all that was being shared throughout the event. I found myself being able to relate to the different topics presented. The Holy Spirit began to bring to my remembrance that it had been a year since I had been off the anti-depressant and I felt that I needed to share this. I did not know any of the ladies that were present, but I briefly told my friend and she told the host. I was given the opportunity to share. I do not remember all that I said, but I stated that depression is real and being a single mother is hard, but I thanked God for allowing me to no longer be on medication. I felt so free after sharing this because even if it did not reach anyone, I knew I could not keep this to myself.

On your journey sometimes, it is good to reflect on where you have been and where you are now. The things you have experienced should be an encouragement and a reminder of what all you have accomplished. It should strengthen you to continue. Also, as you reflect, be careful not to stay too long on the negative things that have happened. It is okay to review, but learn from it, forgive yourself and others and move forward.

Heading into 2014, I am doing it all. I was a working mother going to school and I was also active in ministries at my church: a monthly teacher in children's church, singing in the choir, young adult praise team, facilitating a parent support group and Shepherd's ministry. That summer, I went to Liberty for a week to take an intensive course. Assignments at Liberty were a lot. Somehow, I was able to balance where I could also have somewhat of a social life. During this phase of my journey, I started saying, "Even in my unbelief, I believe." I believed God still performed miracles, I believed God blesses and brings us through whatever our situations may be. I knew God was going to do something grand in my life, but when? I would look at others' lives and see how they were doing great things, but I also knew they had their own journey too. I read a commentary regarding a particular section within the book of Mark, in the Bible where a father of a child cries out, "I believe; help my unbelief" (Mark 9:24). The father is crying to Jesus to ask Him to heal his son who is wrestling with a spirit. As David Guzik states, "He [the father] did not deny God's promise; he desired it." Charles Spurgeon states, "Help my unbelief is something a man can only say by faith."

I felt 2015 was one of the worst years I had lived through. It seemed like things were turning dark and things were just not going the way I wanted. I was unsure of where I was heading, so I attended counseling. At first, I was unsure of why I needed to be there, but it allowed me to have a better outlook on myself. I could tell the devil wanted to see me back on the road of depression, but I was not going down that road. One of the choirs at my church sung a song called, "Amazing" by Ricky Dillard. I really enjoyed the lyrics because they shared the different ways God is amazing. Despite everything that was going on, I would continue to tell myself that God was amazing and I continued doing my best to keep my focus on Him.

That summer, I flew to Liberty again for two weeks to take the last two classes needed to complete my degree. After returning, I went right into interviewing potential supervisors; as I needed to select one for completion of 600 hours for an internship. That August, I began interning while working full-time so basically, I was now working 7 days a week. While I was happy to get closer to the finish line, I knew that this was going to be intense. Almost a year later, in 2016, I completed the internship. It was a proud moment for me because my time mainly was sacrificed. I am thankful that my daughter was able to understand that Mommy was setting out to accomplish something great. By completing my internship, it allowed me the opportunity to focus on her as she was beginning to enter elementary school.

Sometimes, we can take the wrong exit on our journey or we may experience traffic congestion, wondering what happened and why. You may need to take the exit to the rest stop. Why? The rest stop allows you to rest and regroup so you can get back on your journey.

As I approached 2016, things were slowly turning around. I was feeling a little bit stronger and secure. That summer, I took my first attempt at taking the comprehensive exam that my degree required. I felt prepared, but only to find out after a few weeks that I did not pass. I was somewhat upset, but I had two more attempts. I was just ready to finish and obtain my degree.

On the journey of life, you will not always see signs which give you the distance to your upcoming destination. Just know that the light is at the end of the tunnel and trust that it is there. Keep going, keep moving forward.

With full confidence, 2017 was the year of believing for me. I had to come to grips with my choice of whether or not I was really ready to practice believing. After all, in order to live your purpose, you must take action. In February, I retook my exam. While I thought I was prepared again, I did not pass. I remember on the way back home, I was recalling some of the questions I felt I got wrong. Once I looked up the information in my study book, I discovered I had answered them incorrectly. I was disappointed somewhat, but my determination was still there. After taking a two or three-week break from the exam, I got right back to studying again. I knew I had to study a different way to retain the information. I discovered that writing out the information would help me retain it better while studying.

Fast forward to July, it was time for me to take the exam for the third and final time. As it was getting closer to testing, I felt a confidence that I had not felt the previous two times. The Sunday before taking the exam, my dear friend preached a sermon titled, "This Is The Last Time You'll See Me Like This." After she read the Scripture and shared the title, I wanted to let out this holler so bad, because this aligned with my preparation for taking this exam. I BELIEVED I was going to pass it this time. After the service, I had to speak to my friend and let her know this message was for me. I began to cry tears of joy and thankfulness. I had to praise Him in advance. The day of the test, I felt pretty good. On my way to the testing site, I was playing songs of hope, encouragement, and victory. I went inside, took the test and after completing it, I was given a copy of my results. While the results were not final, I BELIEVED that I had passed. August 14th, I received confirmation through e-mail that I had passed! While I believed before this date that I had, my degree was conferred about two weeks later and it felt so good to know that I had finally finished!

For a while, I kept thinking, "How did I make it this far? How did I do it?" I knew it was God's grace and guidance that was with me all the way. He had kept my mind. He gave me peace, protected me and provided. While I had reached this part of the journey, I understood that I had to keep going and reach other destinations. This caused me to start reflecting on my overall journey in life. How have I endured situations as a single mom, on my job, in my relationship with God and others? Several years ago, I said to myself that, "God is beautiful." I learned to look at beauty during the hard times. I had to remember then and still remember now that God's love for me did not change. His provision for me does not change. Having experienced these things and other occurrences in my life, I knew that with my belief and faith being stronger now, that I could conquer anything.

I want to encourage you to learn from each destination you reach on your journey and be able to apply those things as you go after your goals.

Here are my five takeaways lessons learned I would like to share:

1. Embrace the good and bad of your journey. There is a purpose for it all.

2. Do not lose focus on your journey. Spending time comparing yours to others will not get you far. Yes, you can learn from others, but all of our journeys have been tailored made for us individually.

3. "Give God time." —Dr. Rita Twiggs. While we may want things to go our way, God's timing and His way are what's best for us.

4. Enjoy the journey.

5. BELIEVE!

Ashley Dudley

A Texas native, Ashley Dudley holds a B.S. in Dietetics and Institutional Administration from Texas Woman's University as well as a M.A. in Professional Counseling from Liberty University, in which she aspires to become a Licensed Professional Counselor. Ashley is a member of St. John Church Unleashed under the leadership of Dr. Denny D. Davis. A true Servant Leader, Ashley serves in various ministries and has a heart for encouraging others and inspiring them to reach their goals in fulfilling their purpose. Ashley is a member of the National Hook Up of Black Women, Inc., serving as an advocate for women and their families.

Ashley has been a dedicated leader providing staff and parental support ensuring nutrition and wellness for children. Her current role extends that support to schools regarding parental and community engagement. She places a strong emphasis on building both internal and external relationships in order to make a difference in the lives she touches. Ashley is a phenomenal mother to her beautiful and bright daughter, Madison. In her spare time, Ashley enjoys traveling, bowling, swing out dancing, and spending quality time with family and close friends.

To connect with Ashley for future partnerships, speaking engagements, or educational opportunities, reach out to her at *kindra84@yahoo.com*.

Chapter 5

Seasons of Hope
Angela L. Larkin

"May the God of hope fill you will all joy and peace in believing that you may abound in hope."
Romans 15:13

I always imagined I'd be married with a huge family. I remember how I used to daydream about how my life would be as a married woman raising a huge family. At that time, it was all I wanted. I believe God gave me a nurturing spirit which was the basis of my foundation. However, as of today, I am still an unmarried woman whose childbearing years are now in the rear-view mirror. It is certainly not how I imagined my life to be. I did not understand why the path I chose did not lead me to the special relationship that would eventually lead to marriage. Sure, I have had my share of relationships; and some were extremely serious, but never in my wildest dreams would I have ever thought I would still be living a life of singleness in my fifties. What could I have possibly done to have contributed to the failure of these relationships? Was it something I did in my young adult years that was not pleasing to God? Was God punishing me for that very thing? I have always tried to live a holy and sacrificial life, but was that not enough? Okay, so maybe it's not God, but it's me. Was I too controlling or too passive? Could it have been that I was not attractive, interesting or intelligent enough? Did I not express my love and compassion adequately or perhaps, I just wasn't enough? I'm sure one or all these reasons contributed to the downfall of my relationships, right? How do you handle it when things do not go as you planned it?

Let's start at the beginning. I grew up as a middle child to my two brothers. Being the only girl was at times difficult, especially during the earlier years of my life and my siblings didn't make it easier for me. They rarely included me in things that interested them, and they certainly didn't want to participate in anything I was interested in doing. They were good brothers, but there were times when I felt the dark side of loneliness when I was excluded. That was a tough time for me, but my mom was always there to pick me up. We were extremely close then and I'm grateful that our relationship is as strong as ever! Wherever she went, I went because I wanted to be with her. It was like we were two peas in a pod! I suppose the mother-daughter relationship was a natural progression, but it was my father's attention I wanted most. His beliefs and values stemmed from that of a traditional man. He believed girls should spend their time with their mothers and boys with their fathers, therefore it was very easy for my brothers to spend the time that I so desperately wanted to spend with him. I regularly sought after his approval and acceptance of me which felt like a battle inside. Sure, I knew my father loved me, but what I wanted was his time.

After I graduated from college, I found myself spending more and more time with my father. It was as if we were starting a father and daughter relationship for the first time. My most memorable times with my father were when he and I took road trips together. It gave me the opportunity to make up for the times we missed sharing while growing up. The void I felt as a little girl had finally been filled! I wanted him to see how much I'd grown while at the same time, feeling like a little girl inside, who sought his approval. As my father aged, he began to suffer health issues. He fought a good and long fight, but later his life succumbed to his illness. Prior to his transition, God told me to say my goodbyes to my father a week before the doctor instructed my mom to begin calling the family. It was the most difficult thing to do because I knew what God's will was and I had to accept it. So out of my obedience to God, I had to let him go. Losing him to what felt like an untimely death was extremely difficult for me. It was a huge struggle for me and something I didn't quite understand. I internalized it until it became overwhelming for me. It began to affect me in ways I'd never imagined. I was often in a dark place, but no one knew it. I was good at masking my pain all while inside, I was crushed.

While I put on a strong front for my mom and brothers, I was hurting inside. I was broken and I thought: "Daddy, how could you leave me now? You have not met my husband or children to be. Weren't you supposed to wait around for that? Why did you have to leave me now?" I felt a disappointment and very familiar void in my heart and yet, while I knew God was in control, it was still something I had to learn to navigate through emotionally. What helped me through it all was a minister who stood up at my father's funeral and offered some words of encouragement. Knowing that I was still single, he boldly said that God was going to send me someone who would remind me of my father; and that constant memory would sustain me.

A few years after my father's passing, I met someone I thought God had chosen for me. It was perfect. We met in a church setting; the Singles Ministry, and began our journey together from there. He was very charming, intelligent, and good looking! He was a retired officer from the military and was currently working for the government. The first year of our courtship was very intense. He showered me with flowers and gifts, charmed me with his poetry, and always made provisions for me when needed. When he began to include me in his future, I knew then that he was the one for me. This man was no longer a part of my childhood dream; he had become my reality. It was like God finally answered my prayers...or had He?

For seven years, I was on an emotional roller coaster trying to hold on and make what turned out to be an unhealthy relationship work in my favor. Were there red flags along the way? There absolutely were but unfortunately, they did not give me pause. I held on thinking I could love this man enough for the both of us. I even asked God to teach me how to love him at the level where he was and needed to be loved. I tried everything to hold on all the while asking myself, "What's wrong with me?" His disappearing acts were the result of his unfaithfulness which lead to his need to be dishonest. The lies became ridiculously unbearable and while I knew they were lies, I still couldn't walk away in my own strength. He said he loved me and I believed him, but the longer I stayed, the more worthless I felt. How could this be? I held on to the relationship because I thought God called and ordained him to be my husband. How do you let go of what you believed to be sent by God?

This lead me to a state of confusion and conflict with my inner self. Have you ever felt so low that you didn't think you had anything else to live for? As a woman of faith, I never thought it could happen to me and yet it did. You see, after I decided with the help of God, to walk away from what I thought was the promise, I asked myself, "Why? Why would I subject myself to constant disrespect and rejection?" I later realized that it was because I was suffering from low self-esteem and abandonment issues. I held on because I did not think I was deserving of anyone better and I certainly didn't want to feel that sense of loss.

After seeking help, I discovered losing significant family members, including my father and both grandmothers in a small window of time, affected me in ways I'd never imagine. Holding on to something or someone too long or for the wrong reasons were the result of bad choices made in the relationship; which led me to a state of depression. I also learned that I had to address the underlining things that triggered my depression. From my personal evaluation, I discovered I was suffering from abandonment and low self-esteem. As for abandonment, I didn't know how this could be knowing the circle of life will take you through seasons. Biblically speaking, there is a time to live and a time to die. I knew this as a woman of faith so why would I be suffering from abandonment issues? It was all a mystery to me.

Earlier, I mentioned the minister from my father's funeral told me that I would meet someone who'd remind me of my father. At this time, my faith over that prophetic word began to grow weary. Could I trust my heart to make all the right decisions this time? Now I want to share with you about the love of my life. He and I initially met during our high school freshman year. We were in several classes together, but band class is where I saw him the most. During class, during practice, and at the games. He was a nice looking young man who was very intelligent, quick-witted and friendly. He'd tease me a lot and always bugged me about giving him this one thing. He asked for it repeatedly, "Come on, just give it to me. Let me have it.

Can I have your phone number?" He'd often tell me that he used to ask me every day for it and while that wasn't the case, it sure did feel like it! I turned him down so many times, I believe he stopped asking for it.

Sixteen years later he reached out; and this time, after corresponding via social media, he asked me for my phone number and I obliged him. He wasn't the same guy I met in high school; but then again, I wasn't the same girl. We had both grown, and by the grace of God, He gave us another chance to truly get to know one another. While in our adult years, it was as if we were reliving our high school years all over again. We would talk and laugh on the phone until the wee hours of the morning. I'd never felt like I could be anyone but myself with him. From then on, I became his Sunshine. He would always ask if I knew why we met and then he'd remind me it was because he prayed and asked God to send him someone to spend the rest of his life with. Not knowing who that would be, it so happened to have been me. When I asked why he nicked named me Sunshine, he said because I was like a light sent from above which illuminated his world every time he thought of me.

I remember the first time he visited me, it was around the Christmas holidays and I was sick with the flu. He begged to come over for a visit. I gave in and let him come over. I looked a mess, but he didn't care. Shortly after his arrival, I began coughing uncontrollably. He knelt in front of me asking what I needed him to do to make me feel better. As I was about to get up for a glass of water, he told me to stay put and immediately walked into the kitchen, brought me the glass of water and he cared for me the rest of the evening. He'd never been over to my house, but he checked all the cabinets until he found the glasses. Now I had known about his hard shell on the outside, but that night I saw something different. He was so caring, charming and comical. As sick as I was, I totally enjoyed his company. I think that was the night I fell in love with him. It may not have been much, but it was enough for me. My mom was visiting me that day and as he was about to leave, he asked if he could meet his "mother-in-law". I chuckled, thinking how cute it was that he said that and called my mom into the room. After their introduction, my mom, who has always been a quiet and shy person extended her hand to shake his. After he saw that, he quickly said, "Oh no, I'm a hugger." He then extended his arms to give her a gentle hug. I think that night my mom gave him the stamp of approval which made me love him even more. That beautiful ending to a beautiful night was truly the beginning of a beautiful relationship.

Now, this time God has truly answered my prayers. Never in a million years would I ever think he and I would be dating but as fate would have it, we were. We spent more and more time getting to know one another as our relationship deepened. He reminded me so much of my father in many ways. It was his character, mannerisms, and family values that gave me confirmation that this relationship was the one the minister spoke of. It was true, and it would be forever.

Four months later, I noticed something different with his physique. He'd lost an extreme amount of weight. Each time I asked him about it, he'd tell me that his weight fluctuated often and it was not anything to be concerned about. I wanted to believe him but something deep down inside told me otherwise. I pleaded with him to have it checked out, but he never took heed to my requests.

Two months later, I accompanied him to his doctor's office where he received devastating news. It was something that would bring him to his knees. He was diagnosed with terminal cancer. He was hurt, angry and disappointed. I think anyone would feel that emotional pain and more if they received the same news. That blow changed the course of our relationship. What do you do when everything you prayed for, your hopes and dreams suddenly take an alternate course? I thought we had forever, but we didn't. Although we both were people of faith, and fully aware of God's power and ability to heal, it still felt like we were no longer living for the future; but for the right now. I tried being strong for him in his presence and I know he was doing the same around me but, I'd feel his pain each time he was in agony and it broke me.

Six months later from the time he received his prognosis, the love of my heart transitioned from the land of the dead to the land of the living. A man who brought so much joy and laughter into my life will always be remembered. He was my best love and friend and he is now resting safely in the master's arms. After we started dating, we both declared 2015 would be our year. As difficult as it was to lose him, it was still a good year because I got to spend it with him. As for him, he is resting in a better place where he will no longer suffer in pain, where every day is howdy, howdy and never goodbye. I don't think it can it get any better than that, do you? I thanked God for bringing him into my life and even though it was for a little while, I was still grateful. I know in this life he or my dad could never come back to me, but there will be a time when I can go to them in paradise when God ordains it.

My story is a story of love, loss, and hope. These relationships took me on paths of uncertainty and while it was not how I planned or imagined them to be, there were lessons to be learned. It is my prayer that through my experiences, you will be elevated, encouraged and established in your seasons of hope.

What lessons did I learn from my past relationships?

1. When relationships do not go as you hoped or planned, you have to relinquish those plans to God and seek Him with a heart to receive what He has for you. Sometimes we can take a portion of what God has revealed or given to us and make it our own. It is only when we choose not to manipulate His plans will we receive the fullness of it.

2. Loving yourself and speaking positive affirmations will strengthen your self-esteem. Doesn't matter how you feel inside or look on the outside, you must affirm yourself daily. Without this solid foundation, you will find yourself seeking others to validate you through relationships with others.

3. Be self-aware and know that you are valued. Knowing your value will determine when you will walk away from a relationship. I read a quote from an unknown author who wrote, "Just because you love him, doesn't mean you're meant to be hurt by him." God will give you the power and peace to leave if you believe. "God is our refuge and strength, a very present help in trouble." (Psalm 46:1)

4. Being in a relationship with someone who can love you is easy, but does he have the capacity to love you? God revealed to me that the man from the first relationship loved me, but he didn't have the capacity to love me at the level where I needed to be loved. If he is unable to give you more, ask yourself if he has the capacity to give you more. That gave me peace and I knew it wasn't me, but it was him.

5. God is a healer and restorer. Even through our greatest disappointments, God will heal. Losing my best love and friend hurt from the depths of my soul. It reminded me of how I lost my father all over again, but I soon learned that the same God who healed me from the loss of my father would heal me again. He continues to give me strength for today and hope for tomorrow and He will do the same for you. "May the God of hope fill you with all joy and peace in believing that you may abound in hope." (Romans 15:13)

Angela L. Larkin

Angela L. Larkin is a dynamic Christian leader with 20 plus years in corporate leadership. A Fort Worth, Texas native, Angela's purpose is dedicating her life to personal, professional and spiritual growth for women to realize their full potential to make an even greater impact to society. Deemed a servant leader, Angela is affectionately described as compassionate, loyal, and humble based upon her ministry in partnering with women who share in her desire to truly live as God's good and faithful servant.

A Texas Woman's University graduate, Angela earned a Bachelor of Business Administration Degree. While there, Angela passionately developed a solidarity among women from various backgrounds which catapulted her into servant leadership. As a member of St. John Church Unleashed, she is under the leadership of Dr. Denny D. Davis where she continues to develop strong leadership skills through growth in the knowledge and spirit of God. Through her own personal resolve, she shows others the importance of holding on to God's promises that He never leaves nor forsakes us.

In her spare time, Angela enjoys sharing the gospel of Jesus Christ, traveling, and spending quality time with family and friends. To partner with Angela in making a positive difference, she can be reached at *ang_larkin@ yahoo.com.*

Chapter 6

The Joy, The Pain & The Restoration
Erica P. Bolds-Esters

"Trust in the Lord with all your heart and lean not on your own understanding; in all your ways submit to him, and he will make your paths straight." Proverbs 3: 5-6

"If you don't know where you're going, you'll end up someplace else." ~ Yogi Berra

When I look back on my life, I never knew what brokenness, depression, anxiety, or PTSD was. These were topics that were never talked about. As a matter of fact, I don't even think these words existed in our vocabulary. When I was about five years old, I knew that there was something different about me. I was shy, and I clung to my mother a lot. I was also often sad growing up in a dysfunctional home. It was not the best. It was turbulent eighty-five percent of the time and the other fifteen percent, there was peace. There was not much love shown in my family by my father. I knew that my mother loved me because she was always there for me. She never judged anyone, she was a great listener and most importantly, she would tell you the truth and what was on her mind. She never feared anything. She kept it real at all times. I'm so much like her.

My mother was a good woman. She was kind, and she loved her children. My father, on the other hand, would show love one minute and the next minute, he didn't want you to touch him nor did he want to be bothered. Everyone else's kids were the apple of his eye. Why? Because he was cheating on my mother a lot, and she knew; but she also knew within her heart, his day would come and he would have to answer for his sins. Her main concern was making sure that my sister and I were taken care of. My father was not doing it, but he was taking care of his mistress' children, and it was sad that he would allow them to use our department store charge cards with both my parents' names on them. Who does that? What's so embarrassing is that Fredrick & Nelson called our house and told my mother that some woman just purchased a fur coat and wanted to know if she was given permission to do so. My mother said, "No," but she knew who did. The woman in question should have never been allowed to do it. That ain't nothing but Satan himself.

Many arguments went on as my mother tried her hardest to keep the family together. She had a love for the Lord, and she wanted us as a family to be strong in Christ. She enrolled us in family counseling because she cared enough about us. My father was not down with it, but he went anyway. It was plain to see that my father didn't want to be there. Our family physician put some bass in his voice and said to my father, "This is really serious, and if you care about your family, you will put everything aside and be proactive about keeping your family together; most importantly, your marriage."

"But a man who commits adultery has no sense; whoever does so destroys himself." (Proverbs 6:32)

My father just sat there with the same smug look on his face and had nothing to say. My father hurt us a lot, and we never did one thing to him. I look back and try to remember what I have ever done to him, and the only thing I ever did was talk back to him. Other than that, I had not done a thing to him. Maybe some of the things I may have said to him would cause my mom and dad to argue. My sister also talked back. All I wanted was my father's love. I never received that love, and it didn't help that I was being teased and bullied at school. Some of the kids knew that my father was cheating because he was going around town doing what he wanted to do, and didn't care who saw him. It's very hurtful to have another child tease you about your father's infidelity. What hurt even more, was that I told him about it and he didn't care. Just gave me his smug look. If I knew then about who God really was, I would've stayed close to Him. My mother tried to keep us in church. She knew what she was doing because, in her time, God was all they had. I can remember one Christmas, my father bought us nothing. That really crushed my spirit. When I say that, I'm saying he brought us (the family) nothing. It's true that hurting people hurt people because that's what I did. I had no respect for my father, and I didn't honor him. At times, I didn't honor my mother.

"Children, obey your parents in the Lord, for this is right. "Honor your father and mother," which is the first commandment with a promise: "so that it may go well with you and that you may enjoy long life on the earth." Ephesians 6:1-3

At that time, I was far from it. My heart was filled with so much hatred and negativity. I would put on a front as if I was tough, although I was tough when I had to be. I went about things the wrong way, and I had no care in the world. I didn't care about anything or anyone. I will say the majority of my life, I've lived broken, depressed, sad, hurt and I didn't care about my life. When my parents divorced, I was thirteen years old, and I can honestly say, it was a painful time for me. No matter how much my family was dysfunctional, I could not imagine my parents not being together. I could tell that my mother was glad that it was over; however, she was hurt because she loved my father and would've done anything for him. He knew it too.

My mother knew my father since she was seventeen years old but didn't marry him until later. They married other people, and then they married after their first marriages ended. While my parents were going through the process, I was scared because I didn't know what was going to happen. One day, my father wanted to talk to me, and he asked me if I wanted to come and live with him. I was surprised. I said to him, "What about Mom?" He told me that she didn't want me and she didn't love me. My heart sank. I said to myself, "Why doesn't Momma love me anymore? What did I do?" I didn't know what to feel but complete sadness. I don't know why I did this. I agreed, but why I believed my father that day I will never know. I can recall the day I saw the divorce papers in a file while my father was taking me to a friend's house. I will never forget how heartbroken I was. It seemed as if the world was ending. My father did not want me to see those papers. As I walked into my friend's house, I just fell on the floor in tears. I uncontrollably sobbed and what's so sad is that my father did not have anything to say and he didn't comfort me either. He just drove away.

I didn't realize what was ahead of me. I know that I wanted my father's love, that's for sure. Maybe, I was hoping that things would be different. Boy, was I wrong? Once I was living with my father, he did a complete 360 degrees. It was hell. I have to keep it real. My father treated me like dirt, and if he could get me out of his hair, he would find a way to do so. It made me feel as if I was just a guest or at times, I didn't feel welcomed in the place I was supposed to call home. I felt like the enemy too. Some days were good, but the majority of them were bad. By this time, we were living in the South end and I didn't care too much for it, but for some reason my father loved it. I adjusted, and I can remember the times, I was left alone at night all by myself. I recall the times I needed help with my homework, and I could never get him to help me. If he had company, he would say, "You're just trying to interrupt me and my company." You would think the woman that was there would come to my defense. Nope; nothing. Then I asked my father for a tutor, and he said, I didn't need one. Constantly getting shut down by him, I felt defeated. I started failing in school, skipping and going off campus to smoke weed and drink. My father didn't know what I was doing because he didn't bother to check. When the letters would come in the mail from school regarding absences and grades, my father wanted to get angry about it. I told him that I asked him for help and for a tutor to no avail. I told him that if I don't have the necessary tools, I will not succeed. Why did he give that smug look?

From that point on, I was a high school dropout. I did nothing but just hung out and partied as much as I could. My father didn't care about what I did. My mother was very concerned, but she couldn't even have a civil conversation with my father before the arguing began. My depression deepened, and I cried many times. It was getting worse, and at the age of sixteen, I tried to commit suicide. It was my first attempt, and it was not the last. I was diagnosed with depression, and not many medications were available during the mid to late eighties. I was given a prescription and started taking the medication. I didn't trust the medication, but I needed some type of relief from all the sadness I felt inside. Not to mention, feeling alone and hopeless daily. I had to hide it for mask's sake. What I'm trying to say here is that I was not the perfect child and will never claim to be. Besides, how can a perfect child be so broken inside? I didn't feel normal. Does that make sense?

Soon after about six months later, I was going back and forth between my parents and that made me feel somewhat better. At my mother's house, I could chill. My mom would cook, and we would talk. One day, I asked her why she didn't love me (I felt her love while I was with her) and why she didn't fight for me. She told me that she just wanted things to be over and that it was really affecting her. I understood, but she told me that the reason why my father wanted me to come to live with him was that he didn't want to pay child support. Now, I see how he switched things up on me. When we finally had moved into our house, we actually stayed with one of his mistresses. Before we moved out of her house, she tried to be my mother and would tell me what I could and could not do. I was thinking to myself, "You are not my mother." Then again, I realized I was in someone else's house, so I stood down because I didn't want any trouble. I remembered what my mom taught me. "Respect your elders, no matter what the situation is."

My mother continued to live in the house by herself until it sold. I recall before she moved out, the pipes in the house had burst, and she had no heat except in the television room. That's the only place she could stay warm.

I knew this because I would come and stay there with her at times. I didn't care how bad things were. There were times when I just wanted to see my momma and spend time with her. Even though I was a high school dropout, my mother continued to encourage me to go back to school or get my GED. It went on deaf ears because I liked hanging out with my friends and doing what we would do and that was smoking and drinking. It seemed as if my father and I moved a lot. We still stayed in the South end, but this time, we were on the hill. Man, it was a long bus ride going to see my friends.

My father would take me to see my mom, but by this time the house was sold and my mother got her own place. Finally, my father would come in to see my mother and check on her, and I'm glad that they kept it cordial. There were no arguments, just respect. I just thought of something; my grandfather was a minister, and I never met him because he passed away before I was born. He was a good man from what I understood. He warned my mother not to marry my dad because her life would not be good. It makes me wonder why my dad was the way he was, but just because you're a minister's son does not mean that you followed the rules growing up. What happened to my father during his life? What did he go through being a World War II Veteran? I remember my father saying that the devil made him do it, referring to him being married to my mother and cheating on her. You know what? I was not buying it. I told him that he made a choice to do what he did and that my mother loved him so much that she would've done anything for him. However, the enemy stole and demolished my parents' marriage. My father allowed the enemy in by giving him just a little crack to get into.

"The thief comes only to steal and kill and destroy; I have come that they may have life, and have it to the full." John 10:10

The enemy did just that. My father must not have known the second part of this scripture. If he did, he didn't accept it. Our family often went to church, and I recall wondering how we as a family, could have let the enemy in. One thing after another began to happen to us. My sister went on a downward spiral as she became addicted to crack cocaine. The eighties were something else. Crack was the thing back then and her addiction was the icing on the cake. My parents didn't understand. I tried to tell them that my sister was hooked, but they were in denial. She couldn't do any wrong in their eyes. Every time something happened, it seemed as if we became even more dysfunctional. We knew what we needed to do to make things better, but the only one that was not willing to cooperate was my father.

I made a choice to go back to school, and I was excited. My actual year of graduation was 1987, but I was going to be a senior in the class of 1989. Although the thought of graduating was exciting, it ended up not happening. I got caught up going back to doing things that seemed to be more important than school. My father was getting a little irritated which was understandable. He said I needed to do something with my life and I agreed. Being a high school dropout, I just didn't know what I wanted to do. I didn't have any dreams or goals set. It really caused me to think about my reality.

Shortly after our discussion, I received a letter from social security that mentioned I would be getting some money. I didn't understand why but I had received the check and it was about thirty-six hundred dollars. Being a teenager, this was a lot of money to me, and I was so excited. My father told me that I should let him keep the money in his account at the bank, so I did. One day, I went into the city and went shopping. I took my friends (who I eventually found out weren't truly my friends) to lunch and dinner. It seemed as though I was living like, as my mother used to say, "High on the hog." After a few days, I went to ask my father how much money I had left because I wanted to buy a car. His reply was, "What money?" I said to him, "You know what money." I thought he was playing games, but he replied back, "There is no money." I said, "Come again?" He said, "There is no money, you owe me." I said to him, "Owe you? What are you talking about?" He replied, "Just what I said." This man had stolen all of the money that I received from social security, and I began to think of all of the purchases I had made that was going to bounce. That same old smug look appeared on his face again, and he had not a care in the world about what he had done.

I was so stunned that I couldn't even cry. Filled with anger, all I could do was just sit there. I felt robbed and defeated thinking, "Who does that to their children?" I never understood at that time, but now I know that my father was being controlled by the enemy. He knew it and didn't care. I told my mom, my sister, and my friends what happened and my mother asked me, "Why did you let him have that money? Why didn't you call me? I could've kept it for you and you know I would've never done that to you Erica." I know for sure that I could trust my mother, but I thought I could also trust my father. I should have known better back then. I wanted to crawl under a rock and never come out ever again. I tried to see what social security could do for me, but they told me since I allowed my father to put my money in his account, there was nothing they could do, and it was out of their hands. I couldn't believe the money was gone in just a week and a half. I was so mad at myself for trusting my father. I still have trust issues today, but I'm letting God work on me in that area of my life. I want you all to know when you're going through something, let God work on you because He can cleanse you from the inside out and make you brand new.

"Cleanse me with hyssop, and I will be clean; wash me, and I will be whiter than snow." Psalm 51:7

You just have to trust Him and keep your faith strong in Him no matter what it looks like and praise Him anyhow. He loves it when we praise Him. It makes Him happy. I finally made the decision to do something with myself, and I signed up to go to Job Corps. It was May of 1988 when I ended up in Astoria, Oregon which was a small city near the mouth of the Columbia River and off the coast of Oregon. I went there to obtain a trade and receive my GED. I had fun times there, but I would get homesick at times. There were times that I spent certain holidays there if I was not able to go home for a visit. I stayed focused, and I received my GED and a trade in about a year and a half.

Being away from my family was good for me because I felt like I was free of a lot of pain, hurt and disappointments. When I was home for a visit, the dysfunction was still there and sometimes, I could not wait to get back. I had some trials and tribulations there, and I got through them, but I don't know how I did because God was not a part of my life then. Before I graduated, I also did an internship for the 1990 Goodwill Games in Seattle. It was a great experience, and I will never forget the people that I learned from. From a former NBA player, with the Seattle Super Sonics and "Downtown Freddie Brown," who happened to be a great inspiration to all of us. Once I was finally home, I was excited and ready to roll; but I forgot that I was also back to dysfunction. I worked a few jobs, but they didn't last because I had no confidence in myself to do the jobs. I was back into not working at all and back into the same ole same ole; partying and whatever else I got myself into.

I moved out of my father's house and into my mother's. I knew by being at her house, I didn't have to worry about fighting with my father. I knew that my mother would be all that I needed because she was not about that drama and negativity. She was an encourager, not a downer. Shortly after moving, I got a job close to where I lived and maintained employment. Eventually, I enrolled in broadcasting school and got another job later that would be flexible with my school schedule. I must say that I enjoyed going to broadcasting school because there were a lot of hands-on group projects along with individual projects. After graduating in 1991, I went on to work at a local radio station as a disc jockey. It didn't last long because I ended up getting sick by contracting the chicken pox and viral flu. I was so sick and weak one day that I called my station manager to let him know I was sick and that he needed to get someone to replace me that weekend. He wasn't hearing it. He said that he, "would have the studio sprayed down and disinfected." I told him that I was contagious and that disinfecting the studio does not guarantee that no one will become ill. My mother even tried to explain to him because she was a registered nurse but she gave the phone back to me and he fired me right there.

I felt so worthless. It seemed like when I was doing well, someone would come along and tear it apart. Not only did I feel defeated but I wanted just to give up. At this time, I once again attempted suicide but failed. I ended up checking myself into a place because I felt I was going to lose it. The only person I felt was there for me was my mother. It was my second attempt of suicide. I hated my life and I didn't care about what happened to me. I was a negative person who said nothing but negative things. I just didn't care at this time about anything or anyone. I had lost respect for everything and went back to doing what I knew how to do best. I stayed in the streets. I knew I didn't belong there but I didn't care. I wasn't doing bad things or committing crimes, I was just partying anytime I could. Whether I had the money or not, I could find a way to score.

I'm going to fast forward some. In 2003, I lost my mother and I didn't understand why she passed because she was on the mend. "Trust in the Lord with all your heart and lean not on your own understanding; in all your ways submit to him, and he will make your paths straight" (Proverbs 3: 5-6). I wish I knew about this Scripture back then. I was in a deep depression for about six months where I wouldn't do anything but sleep, eat and smoke weed. I was later in a relationship that was toxic; however, I can truly say that he was there for me. It doesn't excuse the toxicity, but I discovered later on that *God don't bless no mess.*

In 2009, I lost my father, and although it hurt, it didn't hurt like my mother's passing. Both of my parents were no longer here, but I knew I would be okay. I had true family and friends who were there for me, and I will also say that my father and I became closer before his passing. Before my mom passed, she told my father that she didn't think she was going to make it. She was a woman who had a love for the Lord, but she told him that if she didn't make it, to make sure that he took care of their kids and grandkids and to love them unconditionally. I did notice that my father did change some after her passing but often wondered why we became closer after my mother's passing. Was it because of guilt or was it because we were all we had? It was me, dad, my sister, and the grandchildren. I will probably never know, but I will never forget the words my father told me when I was going through something. He told me, "Erica, stop being defeated." I was surprised by that. Yes, my father had given his life back to Christ back in the early nineties, and since then, I have never given up on anything anymore. Sure there were bumps in the road, but I prevailed.

I will never forget that May 22, 2012, at 2:22am, I heard a voice say, "Jeremiah 1." "Jeremiah 1?" I thought I was dreaming so I went back to sleep. Again the voice said, "Jeremiah 1." That prompted me to go and pick up the Bible to read Jeremiah chapter 1. I did and only understood the part that said, "I am to deliver a message that He was coming soon." The only person I knew who could tell me what the rest of the scripture meant was my best friend at that time. She was very knowledgeable in the word, so I called her later that morning to tell her what had happened. She picked up her bible and read through the scripture; she revealed that not only was I told to deliver the message, but I was also called to preach the gospel. I was stunned, and the tears began to flow. I told her that I didn't want to and out of nowhere, her voice became strong and loud. She said to me, "Yes you will!" I was like, "That was the Lord speaking through her to me." It scared me and I said, "For you Lord, I will." I have not looked back since.

I am so thankful that I made the right choice! I have so much peace, but most importantly, I have joy. God gave me grace; so no matter what you're going through, let God be your vessel for all things in your life. He will and wants to cleanse you and clean you up; He will have you looking like "new money." I guarantee it. Let God place His purpose for your life inside of you. All are called, but few are chosen. When you don't understand, God is a counselor, healer, best friend, our father, and so much more. I can honestly say if it wasn't for the Lord, I don't know where I would be. Without Him, I'm nothing. I've learned that I am not the only one who goes through something. We all do but there is someone we can call on and that is the Most High that sits in high places. Will you trust Him today? He just wants your time and a personal relationship with you. He's all that He said He is and I guarantee that your life will be never be the same. He loves you, and you are wonderfully made by Him.

LESSONS LEARNED

1. FORGIVENESS ~ It can be hard but ask God to help you in that area of your life. Trust me, the weight of the world will fall right off your back. Forgive yourself as well.

2. JOY ~ You can have joy! You have to make a choice to have joy. You will feel brand new. With God, nothing can stop God's child.

3. LOVE ~ Learn to love yourself and others around you. Always show the love of Christ and love your enemies.

4. STORM ~ When you're in a storm, pray, surrender it to God, and rest in the LORD. He wants to free you from bondage, life's trials, and tribulations if you just trust Him.

5. SELF CARE ~ When you're focused on taking care of others, make sure you take time out for yourself. This is not selfish by any means. You're protecting your temple, you deserve peace, and quiet. It's like going to have a massage or just a simple mani-pedi.

Erica P. Bolds-Esters

Erica P. Bolds-Esters is a native of Seattle, Washington. Erica is currently enrolled at South Seattle College majoring in communications. She earned a certificate in Broadcasting from the National Broadcasting School in which she ultimately aspires to become a journalist. Erica's English Professor helped her to discover how talented she is in writing poetry and she will be releasing her own book of poetry which is designed to positively impact its readers and catapult them into believing with God all things are possible.

After having given her life back to Christ in May of 2012, Erica has been dedicated to touching the lives of others through her relentless service in church and her community. Erica is currently under the leadership of Bishop Zachary K. Bruce, Sr. at the Freedom Church of Seattle. Erica plans on making an even deeper impact to society by inspiring others to totally and completely rely on God at all times. Erica's personal and educational experience coupled with her love for Christ has unknowingly led others to seek salvation and in turn pay it forward to others in need.

To partner with Erica for future engagements, contact her at *yogibesters@gmail.com*.

Chapter 7

Love Thyself First

Becky S. Carter

*"I praise you because I am fearfully and wonderfully made;
your works are wonderful, I know that full well." Psalms 139:14*

Growing up in a large family you'd think one would be showered with love, affection, and encouragement. I'm the youngest of eleven children and most would think in a family that big there would be plenty of love to go around. I was sometimes considered a spoiled brat because my older siblings pretty much raised me. In my mind, they were my protectors and they made sure no one would hurt me. They watched and cared for me like I was their own child. My parents often showed me love by action and constantly stressed how they provided food and shelter for me and that was love. In the back of my mind, I always felt that was what they were supposed to do. At a very young age, I developed feelings of insecurity and I felt as though I wasn't accepted at times. I often wondered what people thought of me and what they were saying about my clothes, hair, and shoes.

I had family members bully me and talk down about my physical appearance. My father was a tough cookie and was very confident. He encouraged me to be strong and not to back away from anyone. He said as long as they don't hit you, ignore them. He stressed the importance of standing up for myself and to not let anyone walk all over you. My mother on the other hand is probably one of the most humble people you will ever meet. She taught me the importance of humility and she preached humility to a fault. My parents had very hard upbringings. My mother raised her siblings as my grandmother was in and out of the house. My father's upbringing wasn't much better. He talked about his mother but not much about his father. Neither one of my parents graduated from high school. My father had several trades but was known as the town's street pharmacist. He was pretty sharp and could multiply and divide in his head with quickness. My mother was a housekeeper to a Jewish family in town. She endured racism on her job regularly but remained humbled.

My high school years were fun and I spent lots of my time with friends. I played the saxophone in band, but was never really too athletic. My self-consciousness started to really get the best of me when boys began to take notice of my friends and not so much me. They often commented on their shapes and how they had a small waist and a nice round butt. I was not blessed with that shape. I was really thin in high school and according to my family I didn't have a nice shape. I wore glasses and had a Jheri curl. They often commented on how wide my hips were, how flat my butt was, and how big my forehead was. I remember my own sister calling me ugly. I couldn't believe she said it and never really took it back.

My self-confidence was really low pretty much all my life. In middle school, thoughts in my head about myself really started to affect me. I looked for validation in what others thought of me. I was looking for their approval of the way I looked and how I should act. I was outgoing and popular in school, but none of the so-called popular boys really liked me. I was the ultimate "home-girl" that everyone called with their problems, but no one really ever asked me out. Not anyone that I wanted to go on a date with. I had one boyfriend in high school that was a real bad actor. He didn't attend my high school but went to a school about 20 miles north. We met in church and he came from a really good family. They were very involved in the church groups and made sure their kids were involved as well. We started to have conversations on the phone, but that was really it. He too talked about how skinny I was and that I really didn't have a fine shape and he didn't really know why he liked me. When he initially asked me to be his girlfriend, I said "No." He said he had never been told "No" by a girl and I guess you could say I was a challenge to him. He pretty much wore me down with kind gestures like flowers every Sunday after church.

We started to date and I found out early on that he had a dark past. He was involved with drugs and had another girlfriend and baby on the way. I was young and gullible and believed he only loved me until I got the call from jail that he was locked up for murder. I was like wow; I really know how to pick them. He said he loved me but I guess not enough to stay out of trouble. I was kind of embarrassed about getting involved with someone like him but he showed me attention and took me out on dates. It wasn't as if I had a million guys knocking at my door trying to date me. I was no dummy and realized after that phone call that the relationship had to end very soon. I penned one letter to him and that was it. I never wrote him again. My father was an ex-convict and I didn't want to be involved with a criminal.

High school graduation was monumental and I was so happy to be moving on to the next phase of my life. I decided to attend a local community college about thirty miles away because I feared leaving home. Instead of my family encouraging me to spread my wings, it was almost as if they wanted to control my future by expressing all the things that would go wrong if I left the area. My older brother offered me the opportunity of a lifetime. He suggested I move with him and his wife to Burbank and finish college. My brother said I wouldn't have to work or pay bills; just focus on getting my degree. He sincerely wanted to see me do something with my life and move out the small town of Easton. My older sister said, "She's not going anywhere, she's not ready to move away from the family." She spoke for me before I could speak for myself. My sister had a way of instilling fear in me and her own children. She brought up every scenario that could go wrong instead of what could go right.

My parents were elderly by now and I really didn't have much direction on what my next steps should be. They were proud of me because I graduated high school and was now working somewhat supporting myself. A little more guidance from them would have helped me, but I understood they did the best they could raising me. The community college experience was great and I was having a good time growing into adulthood. I was meeting new people and I felt a bit better about myself. I was feeling accomplished and my self-esteem was much better. I still didn't feel as though I was doing my best.

After another failed relationship, I decided to pack my bags and leave Easton once and for all. I applied to a major university about three hours away and found a job in the area. I was scared and my family discouraged the move but I decided to do it anyway. I needed to make a decision on my own. I was in a city of roughly a million people. It was a big switch from the 12,000 population I had grown up in. It was a true culture shock. I was depressed upon arriving and refused to stay in my dorm room because my roommate smoked. I stayed with family about twenty miles away. I often asked myself if I had made a mistake by moving so far away by myself. Each and every day was a struggle and I got lost driving from school, to work, to the grocery store. I was miserable and I cried a lot. I was really down on myself because it seemed as if things were not working out.

I met a few girls that I hung out with from time to time. They were of course very good looking and in my mind, I was the mediocre one and didn't measure up at all. At the time, I wasn't an overweight person but I was certainly bigger than them. I was ashamed to show off my body the way they showed theirs off. They had belly button piercings but I was fully clothed head to toe. At this point in my life, I knew my low self-esteem was real. I eventually stopped going out to the clubs with them and I felt periods of depression I called, "low feelings." When they asked me to hang out, I would make up excuses as to why I couldn't go out. I just was not happy with myself. The negative self-talk I used to convince myself I wasn't worthy really started to affect me. This lasted a while and continued after I experienced another failed relationship which I blamed myself for. I had convinced myself that I wasn't good looking enough and that's why the relationship ended, even though me and this guy dated on and off for years.

College eventually took its toll on me and I gained a lot of weight. I dreaded going home to hear what my family thought of my new body. The comments were horrible to say the least. When I finally returned home to my college dorm I was so relieved. I didn't have to hear about how big and unhealthy I was and that they knew I would gain weight. I was like, "UGH, give me a break people! I work at night and go to school all day," but no one seemed to care about that. The focus was pretty much on my outward appearance and how fat I had gotten.

Graduation seemed as if it would never come. I attended college for one year straight so I could finish before I turned thirty years old. I was finally able to apply for graduation and saw light at the end of the tunnel. Once I walked across that stage I felt so accomplished and in a way, complete. Graduating was a major milestone in my life. The experience left me in tears, but they were tears of joy. I was finally a college graduate after ten long years.

My life seemed to be moving in the right the direction for once. I moved to a new apartment and finally landed a management job at a security company. I had more extra time on my hands and started exercising again. I wanted to lose weight and focus on actually liking myself but the self-doubt continued. My "go to" thoughts were negative ones. I lived in fear and felt as though everything I wanted to accomplish in life was impossible. I took up exercise to lose weight but I gained so much more; I felt mentally healthy. I joined Weight Watchers to help with my eating habits and lost about thirty pounds. I was so happy because again, I had accomplished another milestone. I started to feel more confident in myself and my outward appearance had improved.

Things seemed to be on the up and up for a change. I had a new career and new apartment fully furnished and things were good. I was finally ready to date again but got hooked up with the wrong guy. He was super nice but didn't have any direction and barely had a job. Before I knew it, I had let him move into my apartment. I never let a man reside in my space and deep down I knew the relationship was one-sided. I knew it was a foolish move but I didn't really value my worth at that time in my life. The relationship became a co-dependent one. He paid half the rent and utilities but used my car to get to work every day. After he drove my car in the ground he didn't have any money to help me get it repaired. I had to find rides to work and use my savings to fix my car which eventually fell completely apart. To top it off, he didn't buy me a Valentine's Day gift or take me to dinner. I knew these were minimum requirements in a relationship and I felt as if I was settling for less than I deserved.

My self-esteem had hit an all time low. I realized that being around someone who wasn't driven, had no direction, and could barely hold down a job was actually destroying me. I learned at that very moment, energy is transferable. I demanded he move out immediately and gave him a week to do so.

I needed to wipe the slate clean and start over. I purchased my first new car without a co-signer and I was super stoked about completing a major purchase on my own. A couple months later, I met my husband which is truly the man of my dreams. He's a great friend, provider, and just all around great person. I know for sure he is my soul mate and we were truly meant to be. Our marriage is strong because we have so much in common and both came from big families. Even though I am married to an amazing guy, I still had bouts with low self-esteem and not accepting myself. It was nothing he was doing wrong, but I still didn't like me. We had a lovely courtship and after about eighteen months, we were married. I gained a tremendous amount of weight after we got married. I hated to take pictures and go out around people. I was ashamed that I had let myself get to this point again.

At this time boot camps were the new exercise craze. I was afraid but signed up for one because I so desperately wanted to get in shape and look good again. It was hard at first, but I got results after about a month. I was pleased with the program and continued it for about a year or more. A little bit of the weight came back again, so this time I started cross fit. It was extreme exercise, but I met some amazing people. I injured my ankle and after that it was never really the same. I was determined to make exercise apart of my routine and joined a local gym. The results were not just weight loss but it helped with the negative thoughts I had. After trying all this, I was not totally happy.

I prayed and asked GOD for direction. I wanted to have a healthy mindset and a healthy body. For once I wanted to accept myself no matter what I looked liked on the outside. I knew I had a good heart and people loved me but I wanted to fully love myself. I thought about my life growing up and I often wondered why I didn't have a positive outlook about myself like some of my friends did. I was a loyal friend, good wife, daughter and sister and would give the shirt off my back to those who needed me. I was a believer and was supposed to have faith in GOD, but why was I so afraid of being this positive happy person? I had convinced myself that being happy all the time would make be appear to be detached from reality. This was the furthest thing from the truth. I realized that I wasn't really taught how to be uplifting, encouraging, and supportive to others and actually thought folks felt the same way about me as I did about them. Happiness is truly a choice and I've learned this simple concept the hard way. I had to learn that I was in control of my emotions and reactions.

I considered myself to be a mentor to some and counselor to others. I gave great advice to folks but rarely took it myself. I started to self-evaluate more and learned that I didn't take on new challenges because I was afraid to fail, but because I lacked confidence. These thoughts were all linked back to my childhood. I don't think my family really understood how powerful positivity is for a child. In speaking with me, I would appear to be very well put together; polished, so to speak. I seemed poised and would come off as having a real strong personality, but deep down, I didn't completely love myself. I had gotten to a point where I couldn't even accept a compliment from others and I really wasn't able to give compliments either. When I did receive a compliment, I felt as though it wasn't sincere and I didn't deserve it. In my mind, this was a sign of not being real. If I lifted others up and encouraged them along the way, I thought I was being fake.

I was from a generation of *action-neers*. They expressed, "I'm showing you love through action." Action love is important but verbal love is just as important. I realized I was missing the mark by not expressing to others through words, how I felt about their accomplishments. This way of thinking took me through years of trust issues with new people I would encounter. I would often think new folks I met, were out to get me, sabotage my efforts, or they were just being out right mean. At work, I would let my mind race when comments were made that I didn't agree with. I automatically thought my peers were trying to come after me and make me look bad in front of others. I didn't realize that no one could make me look bad if I hadn't done anything wrong. I defined this type of thinking as the self-sabotaging approach. I was so concerned about what others thought about me that what I thought of myself had no room to flourish.

I realized that no one could change the perception of how I felt about myself but me. I started to read positive books and surround myself with people that had characteristics I was lacking. My prayers became stronger because I was seeking direction from GOD, but I still had a long road ahead of me. I would look at folks who were super confident, and in the back of my mind I was thinking, "WOW, I would never wear that," or "Gosh, they really love themselves." I could never quite wrap my head around how other individuals had the nerve to wear what they were wearing. In the environment I grew up in, I was taught to be ashamed of me. It never dawned on me that I wasn't taught to be proud of who I was. I longed to have that confidence and love for myself because I knew I deserved it.

I was searching for real inner peace and happiness, so I started to write positive affirmations on my mirror every day. I also separated myself from those who spoke negatively about others or had a negative outlook period. My goal was to be so positive that folks would leave conversations with me uplifted. At work, my peers began to say, "You always try to find something positive about every situation." My reply was, "that's what I am supposed to do." I refused to let negative energy into my thoughts. I finally understood that positivity and realism could both exist in my brain. I made a conscience effort not only to work on encouraging others, but started with encouraging myself.

Daily exercise became my release so much that I didn't let days or weeks go by without getting in at least thirty minutes or more a day in the gym; this became a part of my routine. I found myself even working out on vacation and business trips. I felt better when I worked out and defiantly looked better. I set small weight loss goals for myself and worked really hard through diet and exercise to make permanent changes. I dealt with periods of yo-yo dieting, but finally found balance by simply eating right and working out harder in the gym. My real results came through consistency and intensity. The diet changes such as eliminating processed foods made me feel more balanced and energized. Above all, exercise made me feel like I was physically and mentally well.

My focus was to change my physical appearance, but I knew that I had to work on how I viewed myself. During my workout time, I would reflect, talk to GOD and focus on my day. My thoughts were positive during this meditation time, even if something bad was going on. Living a healthy balanced life has become my passion. It's a conversation that I strike up with anyone I meet and I never grow tired of talking about it. I truly believe that health is wealth and God created us all for a purpose. Exercise became my outlet and helped me work through my low self-esteem issues and self-sabotage. My goal is to help others live their best lives by first loving themselves. I encourage you to be happy about you first and do more of what makes you happy and puts you in a positive place. This type of thinking will set the foundation for your entire life. I wish you self-love, peace, and positivity.

Lessons Learned:

1. Believe what GOD says about you. (Ephesians 2:10)

2. Love yourself, but be willing to make character changes if it's going to make you better. (1 Corinthians 13:4-8)

3. Don't compare yourself to others; comparison is the thief of happiness. (Proverbs 29:25)

4. Surround yourself with like-minded people who are going to encourage, uplift, and elevate you. (Luke 6:45; Proverbs 27:17)

5. It starts with you! Encourage yourself and believe you can accomplish whatever your heart desires. (Luke 1:45; Psalms 45:6)

Becky S. Carter

Becky S. Carter is a best-selling, award winning author, leader & entrepreneur. Deemed a "Woman of Influence", Becky propels others to seek their passion which leads to their purpose. Next to serving the underserved, Becky's love for health and wellness is unyielding as she places a deep emphasis on women & children knowing the importance of maintaining a healthy lifestyle through both exercise & food choices. As a result, she's ministered to the reality of "your body is a temple" helping those who struggle in areas of true health commitment to "Flex Their Faith."

Becky acquired a Bachelor of Science Degree in Business Administration from the University of Texas, Arlington in Arlington, Texas. She's Partner/co-owner for A&B Creations, LLC, & Carter Properties, LLC. Becky & her Husband, Frederick have been married for 13 years & they have 2 amazing twin daughters, Adrian & Andrea as well as a precious granddaughter Alanah. Becky is a member of First Baptist Church of Lockhart under the leadership of Dr. Fritz Williams. In her spare time, Becky loves exercising, traveling, & spending time with family and friends. For partnership opportunities, Becky can be reached at *beckyspruell@hotmail.com.*

Chapter 8

My Flares, My Falls, My Faith

Crystal Varner

Jesus loves me this I know
For the Bible tells me so
Little ones to him belong
They are weak, but he is strong

Yes, Jesus loves me for the Bible tells me so"
-Anna B. Warner, 1820 -1915

I remember singing this song in Sunday School as a child. Yes, Jesus loves me. On April 27, 1991, my first child was born. I had a baby girl at 9:43am after being in labor all night. I had no idea how this relationship would blossom. My relationship with my own mother was strained at times. Some of it was because I was a rebellious teenager trying to find my way. Some of it was a no-nonsense mother trying to guide me, but in a direction that I don't think

God intended for me. There is no manual for parenting, so I think we both learned a few things. It got better as I got older. Everything that happens in my life, I believe, happens for a reason.

One day, it was around midnight and I was fast asleep. My husband was out with his friend playing Madden on the PS3. My son was in his room and my daughter, now 21, was out with friends. My phone rang and my daughter was on the other end. She told me that her best friend's mother had been seeing my husband in her apartment complex with one of her female neighbors and they were together at that very moment, but she didn't know where.

I feel my relationship with my daughter is truly blessed by God. She and I share a special bond. She has always been able to share things with me, even personal things. We are mother and daughter, but we are friends as well. She makes me a better person in so many ways. She's kind, funny and giving. Of course, I'm sure every mother says that about their child. Why Lord, would you have her, of all people be the one to call and tell me that my husband, her stepfather and father figure was cheating? Jesus keep me near the cross! Naturally, I got up with a mission...find him! Actually, I waited for him to come to me... kind of. I waited in her apartment complex because when you pick someone up, it's only good manners that you would drop them back off. I wanted to see it for myself. Don't judge me! I know.

Remember the whole woman scorned thing? All common sense and Christian values were in my rearview. Anger had taken over after the shock. Anyway, after a short car chase, me being the chaser, the night ended with his belongings being given to him. Given may be the wrong word, but you get the picture. The next few weeks were a blur.

When I could finally talk to or even look at him again, he suggested marriage counseling. I said, "Fine, but all I want to do is show up. You stay where you're living. You find the counselor. You make the appointments. You pay for it!" And, he did. We went for many sessions. Then he started saying he felt the counselor was on my side. Really? We went weekly, and the counselor continued with his assessment of our marriage. He felt that we should work it out. I continued to pray, studied the Word, and memorized and recited all of the marriage scriptures I could find. "Two people are better off than one, for they can help each other succeed. If one person falls, the other can reach out and help. But someone who falls alone is in real trouble. Likewise, two people lying close together can keep each other warm. But how can one be warm alone? A person standing alone can be attacked and defeated, but two can stand back-to-back and conquer" (Ecclesiastes 4:9-11). My faith would not let me give up on my marriage. Father, your Word says, "We are one flesh. Therefore, what God has joined together, let no one separate" (Matthew 19:6). "He who finds a wife finds a good thing"(Proverbs 18:22).

I was told numerous times by various friends, "Crystal, you have every right to stay, but you don't have to stay." I shared my story with a good friend at church, and she gave me the book, *The Power of a Praying Wife* by Stormie Omartian and shared a little of her testimony about her own marriage. It was a really good read, and my friend's personal story blessed me tremendously. I read and prayed and read and prayed. This book was full of scriptures and prayers for a marriage, but we weren't 1 flesh. God loved me too much to continue to let me be in this mess of a marriage, so after a couple of months of counseling, I knew that my marriage was over. I had fought the good fight, and quite honestly, I was done. The years had taken a toll, my own daughter had to call me and tell me that he was cheating, and I was done. I told him I wanted a divorce. To be honest, I really don't think he believed me...but I was serious. I had prayed about it. I had peace about my decision. I deserved better. It was over. It sounds very simple and final, doesn't it? Well, it wasn't. It was just beginning. So I began to get the paperwork together, while at the same time, he decided to move to North Carolina. He had decided he was not going to give me a divorce. He would not give me his address. He wouldn't give me his employer. All I had was a phone number. I continued to pray and pray because I needed and very much wanted this divorce. My sister asked me, "Are you sure? You don't have to get divorced." I told her that I wanted a divorce because I wasn't going back, and I could not close this chapter of my life without it. I feel like, as African Americans, we break up, but sometimes don't take the final step and I needed closure. I had a few people disagree, and that was okay.

I was at my wit's end. Every step I took, there was an obstacle. Lord, all I wanted was out of this marriage. The mental anguish of fighting, waiting, and wanting to get out of the marriage, paying bills alone, raising two children, getting a daughter through college, people at my job acting like they had lost their minds, and the physical pain was weighing on me. "Lord, why?" I asked. Yes, I know I was selfish to ask "Why?" But then I thought, "Why not me?" One night, as I was balled up in the fetal position, I even remember asking God if He was going to let the enemy kill me. I was praying and weeping and every joint in my body was hurting down to the small joints in my fingers and toes. I was so tired. I couldn't sleep because every time I drifted off to sleep, I was awakened by the pain whenever I made any type of movement.

I don't know about anyone else, but when things happen to me, I start to do a self-examination. Maybe I shouldn't have done this, or maybe that thing I did in 1972 is coming back to haunt me. "It's karma, I'm reaping what I sowed." Okay, I'm exaggerating. I was two years old in 1972, but you get the picture. "But I go to church. I sow. I pray. I go to Bible study. I have a personal relationship with you, Lord." Have you ever felt like you were alone and couldn't feel God?

My hair started coming out every time I combed or touched it. My joints would hurt so bad. I was stressed. I went to the rheumatologist. He was concerned, so he put me on some antidepressants and gave me a steroid shot in the butt. Yes, it's as humiliating as it sounds, the antidepressants made me feel numb, absolutely numb. I felt nothing; not happy, not sad, not angry…Nothing. I just didn't feel like myself.

If you're lost and wondering how I ended up seeing a rheumatologist, let me take you back a few years to Greensboro, North Carolina. I think it was 2003. The pain in my joints hurt so bad. I woke up one morning after a restless night and called the doctor's office and said, "My name is Crystal Varner, and I would like to make a doctor's appointment. I know my doctor is not available today, but I will see anyone. This pain is almost unbearable. This medicine is not helping my pain, and it makes me drowsy. I can't work drowsy." A few hours later, I'm in the doctor's office describing the pain and lack of relief, and he says to me, "You're very young to be in so much pain. Let's run some tests." Well, that was no shock. I've had arthritis for over three years now. Blood work is my life, right? I receive some pain meds, and then I go home. A few days later, I received a call, and they need to run more tests. Okay, I shrug my shoulders. I'm back and sitting in the chair and as they draw blood, I ask the nurse, "What are you testing me for?" She says, "Lupus and some other things."

I thought, "Lupus!?!?!?" Then she says, "Your previous tests for arthritis came back negative." My next thought was, "Negative? What does that mean?" After having my blood drawn, I immediately called my uncle and aunts in South Carolina, and we started praying. "But he was wounded for our transgressions, he was bruised for our iniquities: the chastisement of our peace was upon him; and with his stripes, I am healed" (Isaiah 53:5).

At my next appointment, I had my husband, two aunts, my uncle, and a cousin there to support me. And… my tests were positive for lupus with a connective tissue disorder. I didn't even know what that was. After my appointment, we went to IHOP and had, "All You Can Eat Pancakes." It's funny, the things you remember when you're going through something. Everyone went home, and I began my drive home and stopped at the red light. During my stop at the red light, I thought about all the things I had read about lupus. "Oh my God! Lord help me. What in the world? Lord, why have you forsaken me?" It took me so long to pull myself together, I had to pull into the gas station. I didn't know anyone with lupus. I began crying, praying and reciting healing scriptures because, at that moment, my body just hurt! I needed to feel the love of God. "Yes, Jesus loves me. Yes, Jesus loves me. For the Bible tells me so."

After a few weeks of taking the antidepressants that the doctor prescribed for me, I couldn't do it anymore. I didn't like the way they made me feel. I was still going through the motions just without any emotions. I continued to pray. Praying while broken. Fighting the good fight. Months passed. God sent me who I needed when I needed them. My children, the friends, and the mentors that He placed in my life during this time were priceless. I remember months before any of this happened, I needed to choose which

Victorious Disciples class I would take next. I had taken Victorious Disciples Parts One and Two. I decided to take *One-On-One Mentoring* as my next class. My mentor, Rene, was truly a blessing during this time in my life. I could call her anytime, and she was that sweet, encouraging, gentle voice in my ear quoting scriptures and letting me vent. My friend, Mary, shared her testimony about her marriage with me, and it gave me the encouragement I needed to continue. I didn't tell the rest of my family about the state of my marriage until after almost a year of separation. With them being in South Carolina and me being 1100 miles away in Texas, I didn't want them to worry. One day God said, "It's time," so I called and told each of them.

Did I mention that I'm the oldest of my mother's three children? I'm almost 13 years older than my baby brother. I babysat, bathed, dressed, cooked and cared for him when he was young. My mother died when I was 30, and he was 18. My father passed the year before her. One day my brother called me for $100 to purchase some clothes for his new construction job. I said, "Sure, it's on the way." That was the last time I spoke to him before all hell broke loose. I don't even remember how I found out that he had been arrested. I just remember being on the phone with his attorney and his children's mother, a lot. "Ten years?! Oh God, why Lord?" He accepted a 10-year plea deal. This sent me back into an emotional roller coaster, so the pain was back. No amount of Tylenol, Motrin, Advil or Aleve even touched the pain. My doctor and many before him told me they didn't want me on steroids; however, they knew it was the most efficient way to attack the joint pain during a severe lupus flare, and I needed another shot. "Yes, it was in the butt!"

One day, I found out that I could take out an ad in the local newspaper where my husband lived and if he didn't reply, I would not need his "permission" for the divorce. So, I decided it had been long enough, and I was doing it. I still prayed. Before I could take the ad out, he called and I asked him for his home or work information again so I could have him served with papers. His reply was, "I'm not giving you a divorce." Then determination turned to anger, and anger turned to fury. My reply was straight to the point and direct. I told him, "Nice Crystal is gone. It has been months, and I have been trying to be nice, but I see I can't be. You will give me a divorce, even if I have to subpoena every one of your friends that were in cahoots with you during all your dirt and have them testify!" I'm sure I am leaving out a few adverbs and adjectives. I started naming names and taking no prisoners. He gave me the address to his home that day. I thanked God. The craziest thing is the first thing I said to myself is, "You said what you needed to say, and he didn't take you out of your element. You didn't curse once." Anyone that really knows me knows I don't curse. However, if you knew back in the day (in Brooklyn or at Benedict College) or BMC (before my children) Crystal, she cursed all the time.

This was a huge accomplishment for me. I had him served and waited for his reply. I went to court. He didn't show up! I left that courtroom a free woman. I attended divorce counseling at my church. This blessed me so much because the couple facilitating the classes were a married couple that had both divorced and remarried.

Even after my whole ordeal, I have grown to have so much respect for the union of marriage because of the teachings that I received while I was a member at Cedar Grove Baptist Church and St. Johns Baptist Church. It is not a union that I take lightly. It is a union ordained by God. I was divorced with a son graduating high school, and I was ready to come back to the East coast. Virginia, here I come…once I get a job.

I believe that we get in familiar situations; whether they are good for us or not, they are familiar, and we get comfortable. Sometimes, God must take us out of our comfort zone. I don't know about anyone else, but I am such a creature of habit. If it's working why fix it? How many of us know that God doesn't operate like that? And I like control. There goes my transparent moment. And again, God doesn't operate with us in control. Honestly, that's one of the main reasons I don't drink. I got tipsy once when I was young. I felt I had given my control over to a bottle of Cisco and I never got tipsy again. After my marriage was over, it was like God whispered, "For I know the plans I have for you," declares the Lord, "plans to prosper you and not to harm you, plans to give you hope and a future. Then you will call on me and come and pray to me, and I will listen to you. You will seek me and find me when you seek me with all your heart" (Jeremiah 29:11-13).

I was ready to leave Texas and get back on the East coast closer to my family. A prior co-worker contacted me about a position at the child care corporation that he was working at in Virginia, but they weren't willing to pay for my relocation. I accepted a position as Regional Manager with a different corporate child care company making about $10,000 more than what I was making in Texas. I had been in Virginia for about 6 months and the company that I had initially interviewed with contacted me. That position came with another raise and a nice car allowance. Look at God! He made up for that lost income, and I was able to put both of my children through college. It was honestly like once my divorce was final, God started opening doors for me that I could have never opened on my own or imagined. Won't He do it?

One of my girlfriends and I always say, "Hindsight is 20/20." Now, when I look back, I have to say it was probably during this ordeal that made me feel the love of God most prevalent in my life. When I look back now at "one" of the most difficult trials in my life, I still feel His love and His carrying me through each of these trials. It was only through his grace and love that I was able to come out of this situation with my sanity, a greater love for myself, a greater understanding of marriage, and a greater understanding of His love for me. He sustained my health through this. I have not had to have a shot in years. That's definitely not because I haven't been through trials since then. They haven't come up with a cure yet and it's still the most effective way to remove the pain; however, God has kept me through my flares and my falls, and I'm thankful. Talk about love, life and lessons learned.

Here are five of the lessons I've learned:

1. F- First and foremost, family and friends are important. I don't know that I could have made it through some of these things if it weren't for my family. Invest in your relationships. Surround yourself with positive people. Your clique matters. Surround yourself with people that love you and have your best interests at heart.

2. A- Accept, embrace and celebrate change. The one thing in life that's constant and guaranteed is change. I have learned to accept, take on, and commemorate change. Let go and let God.

3. I- If God brought me to it, He will bring me through it. God is omnipresent (present everywhere), omniscient (all knowing) and omnipotent (all powerful). Even if you can't feel him, know that He is there.

4. T- Trust my gut. Some things just aren't meant to be. Take things one day at a time, one step at a time.

5. H- Hibernating is necessary sometimes. Spending time alone puts things into perspective for me. Whether it is reading, singing, writing, praying, meditating, or cooking I enjoy my alone time. And a good night's sleep is a gift. It gives me clarity.

Crystal Varner

Crystal Varner is a leader, manager, and director with greater than 25 years' experience in early childhood education administration. She is highly skilled in the facilitation of cognitive, language, social, emotional, and the physical development of children. Crystal has a broad range of professional training which is used to strengthen the platform for awareness of the special needs of children.

Crystal acquired her Bachelor of Arts – Early Childhood Education Administration degree from Ashford University & is currently pursuing her Master of Arts in Organizational Management. Crystal is a Woman of God who has served in various capacities of ministry as a means to strengthen her walk with Christ all while leading others to reignite their own personal relationship with God.

Crystal is a member of St. Paul's Baptist Church, Richmond, Virginia under the leadership of Dr. Lance Watson. She is the mother of two amazing children, Rasheed and Shante. In her spare time, Crystal enjoys reading, writing, and traveling. To connect with Crystal for partnership opportunities & future engagements, email her at *caulder.crystal@yahoo.com*.

Chapter 9

Forgiving My Mother Healed My Womb
Latannia Locks

"Bear with each other and forgive one another if any of you has a grievance against someone. Forgive as the Lord forgave you." Colossians 3:13

My mother is a beautiful woman with beautiful brown skin that's always glowing. I've never seen a pimple or blemish on her baby soft smooth skin. Alike, I am admired most outwardly by how beautiful my skin is. I always give credit to my mom for that part of her that she's given me. Her great skin is not the only part of her that I inherited. My mother has a big heart and will give you her last if she had to. Our hearts alike, are just as beautiful as our skin. Somewhere along the way, my mother's heart was broken; and unlike her skin, it left blemishes, bruises, and scars. I don't think her heart has ever been repaired or restored back to its proper functioning way. I've never seen my mother truly happy. Of course, I've seen her smile, but it was only to disguise the pain and shame she felt for being a failure. Failure at never becoming a wife, her best self, high school graduate and worst of all; failing at motherhood. My mother would never admit that. I don't believe any woman sets out to get pregnant, go through nine months of carrying another soul, intense labor pain, delivery of the baby and say, "Well, now that I've given birth, I'm just going to sit back and watch this whole motherhood thing unfold and fail."

"Therefore, there is now no condemnation for those who are in Christ Jesus." Romans 8:1

I believe that my mother needlessly condemned herself for past failures and continues to walk in guilt and shame. That guilt and shame is keeping her from experiencing the best part of herself and a daughter who's waiting to love and embrace every flaw. I'm not my mother's only daughter. In fact, I have two other sisters and nine brothers. I would like to think that with each child, my mother wanted to do better, but just didn't know how. Out of my sisters, the relationship my mother and I have is hard to explain and I'm sure by the time this book is released, nothing will have changed. Let me start by saying, "I Love My Mother and nothing will ever change that. Not even her." For the sake of the length of my chapter, I'll jump to where I think the big disconnection really began for my mother and me. But first, please keep in mind that I'm not here to bash my mother, but only here to share my story and hope it helps someone else. Also, keep in mind that she's not all to blame because my father wasn't any better than she was and I truly love them both.

I felt like my mother chose her boyfriend over me. No, the truth is, my mother did choose her boyfriend over me. For a long time, I struggled with the thought of how first, a mother, my mother could so easily choose a man over me.

To make matters worse, she had one that meant her and her kids no good. Every chance he got, he beat the life out of her. She met the better half of my sibling's dad when I was five years of age. We moved in with him, and life became a living hell for us all. He yelled, screamed, cussed and fussed all day long. My mom didn't work, and he did odd jobs that paid him under the table. We didn't have much of anything and sometimes just keeping a roof over our head wasn't a sure thing. We moved from one house to another it seemed like every other month. Things were very unstable for us. One thing I can say is that we were never homeless. We never lived on the streets, but the hell we caught in the living conditions we were in; the shelter may have been a better choice. Because of government assistance such as WIC and food stamps, we never went without food. Whether it was a sugar sandwich or a syrup sandwich, we had something to eat.

It wasn't long before he started to beat her just because that's what he felt like doing. Some years had gone by and my mother endured a lot from him physically, mentally, emotionally and spiritually. He broke her spirit into pieces. He had power over her that left her lifeless, breathless and hopeless. He kept her away from her family and dared any of them to come around where we lived. As a kid, it was so painful to watch my mother be so helpless. My kid mind couldn't understand why she couldn't just leave. Take us and leave him. I remember times when she would bring him his plate of food and hand it to him, only for him to literally throw it in her face, call her names and then jump on her beating her with his fist leaving visible bruises and scars that never healed. He would wake me up at 4 a.m. in the morning to go and wash dishes and would walk through the kitchen exposing his genitals to me. It went from exposing himself to me, to finding his way out of the bed that he and my mom shared, and into a room where I shared a bed with two other siblings.

The first time I felt him touch me, I knew it was wrong. I told my mother what he did, and she may have fussed at him, but nothing serious happened. I'm not sure if she didn't believe me or if she didn't want to believe it was happening. It happened over and over again. He never penetrated me, but one time he paid me 5 dollars not to tell my mom that he had been touching my vagina the night before. He may have had some supernatural power over her, but when it came to me, God was not having it. He was still there when I gave her the "hush" money. I told her what he did and what he said. For a moment, she was actually mad about it. I thought Mama Bear had finally stood up to protect her cub. She even called the police. But what happened when the police got there sent me into a deep depression. Once again, she failed me. By the time the police arrived, he was already gone. I was standing on the other side of a 6 foot screen door when I heard the officer ask my mom, "What's going on?" To hear my mother say, "Oh, nothing. Everything is alright now," made me weak. I remember thinking, "This was our chance to get help, to get out. No more of him touching me and beating you. No more of my brothers waking up in the wee hours of the night to him beating them with a water hose, extension cord, or belt buckle. No more having to pretend to be doing housework when he's home so that we don't get beat. No more of his son coming over trying to force his penis in my mouth while I'm trying to sleep. No more sleepless nights because I'm trying to stay awake to protect myself." Unfortunately, that day we didn't get the help we needed, and the abuse continued.

I was around 8 years old at the time when I became very ill. I lost my appetite for any food or beverages. I begin to vomit bile and had the worst pain ever in my right side. I was living this way for about a week or so, and to no fault of my mother, she thought maybe I had a stomach virus. But it wasn't until I started throwing up bile and I could no longer walk or barely crawl, that my mother called a cab and rushed me to Charity Hospital in New Orleans, LA. I couldn't make it through the hospital sliding doors fast enough before I was put on a rollaway bed and rushed to the emergency room. My appendix perforated, spilling infectious materials into my abdominal cavity. Because I had gone so long before being treated, the doctor that looked over me that night told my mother if she would have waited any longer, she would have lost me before the break of dawn. The poison had so badly affected my blood that my stay in the hospital was longer than anyone would have expected. I was there so long, my mom brought me a TV to watch. I couldn't walk on my own for weeks at a time and had tubes down my nose that were draining the infection. Though I was in pain and agony and for crying out loud, lying in a hospital bed; I actually enjoyed being there. For that moment, I no longer had to deal with physical or sexual abuse. I didn't feel scared to fall asleep because I feared I would be touched inappropriately. I didn't have to witness my mother's verbal and physical abuse by the hands of the man that claimed to love her or look after my siblings while my mother left the house. I could finally feel like a kid with no worries. I could laugh and not get yelled at for simply laughing. I didn't have to go to school and be teased and bullied by my peers and my 4th grade teacher for having short nappy hair due to a relaxer breaking it all off. I felt free, but that freedom didn't last long. I knew I would have to go home sooner than later.

Turning Point

It would take another year before God would send me help by way of me helping my mother. One night as I stayed awake, I thought to myself that if he hits her one more time, I'm going to kill him. I was so angry and developed so much hate in my heart for this man that I no longer wanted him alive. He brought misery to us all. He hated me from day one. He was never a father figure and never tried to be one. He was selfish, arrogant and a snake. For the life of me, I couldn't understand how my mother could love the scum of the earth. One morning, I was leaving for school. As I was walking out the door, I heard a loud bang, and a loud, terrifying scream followed. I ran back to where I heard the noise and what I saw with my eyes, I would never want to have to witness again. She was down on the floor in between a deep freezer and the refrigerator begging for her life. I could no longer bear the sight of him anymore. I picked up a glass bottle and went straight for his face. I ended up cutting him over his right eye. He needed stitches to repair the damage. The way he was punching her, I was afraid for her life, and before he takes her life, my thought was to take his.

I was only 10 at the time, but I'd had enough of the abuse. At that moment, my life changed; and my relationship with my mother would never be the same. After cutting him across the eye, I ran to the next-door neighbor for help. I told them what was going on and asked could I use their phone to call my grandmother. I stayed there until my grandmother came for me. I took nothing with me except for the clothes on my back and the shoes on my feet. I never went back to that house again. I never lived with my mother again after that day. I did miss her and I longed for her many days and nights. I visited her from time to time, but nothing permanent. I don't feel that my mother abandoned me; I truly feel in her own way, she thought she was protecting me by letting me go. I don't think she felt it would change everything.

Love

My mother and I have a very estranged relationship. As of today, we don't speak. Believe me, I have tried my best to build a relationship with her for many years. At times, it seemed as if we were going to be okay, but it never stuck. I don't understand why she continues to push me away and some can't understand why I keep holding on. One, it's because I love her and no matter how old I get, I will always love and need her. I needed her when I got married, and she wasn't there. I needed her through those difficult times when I was trying to get pregnant and when everything felt like it was falling apart. Those times when something really great happened like; when I made my first batch of gumbo from scratch, or when I kept a real plant alive for more than two weeks, or on a more serious note, when I was diagnosed with PCOS (polycystic ovarian syndrome) and thought I would never be able to give birth to my own kids.

Whether a good or bad mother, we love our mothers so much because they are the first and most important people in our lives. They gave birth to us. It's a child-like innocence to long for a mother who loves everything about you wholly and completely. It is normal to want to lay your head on your mother's shoulder and feel the safety and well-being of her love and compassion. To envision her saying, "Baby Girl, I'm always here for you." We all need more than the necessity of a roof over our head, food, and clothes to wear. The magnitude of the unconditional love of a trusted, loving mother and father can never be underestimated. Parents are supposed to be the inspiration

LOVE, LIFE & LESSONS LEARNED

in everything we do, and we hold them to it. I never got that from my mother, but I do have the gift to give it.

Life

I have been through a lot in life. From feeling abandoned by my mother and father, raped at a young age by a neighborhood boy (but didn't tell anybody because I felt like nothing would happen), robbed at gunpoint at the age of 11, looked for love in all the wrong places, and many other things. I was counted out by family members. They said I would be pregnant by the age of 13, but that didn't happen. I should have been a statistic. God had other plans for my life. I never felt like I belonged in the environment that I grew up in. Even when I lived with my grandparents, which was better than my prior home, we lived in one of the worst projects in New Orleans, LA. Crime on top of crime. I witnessed murders by gunshot wounds and beatings to deaths with baseball bats. Police would raid our house because they thought we ran a drug house. We lived among crack heads and dope dealers, prostitutes, and pimps. No wonder they counted me out. My older brother fell victim to the drug gang and lost his life shortly after turning 18 years old. My father couldn't be a father because of his drug and alcohol addiction.

Though I had the best grandparents, I still had to grow up fast and figure life out on my own. I had no time to just be a kid. I'm thankful for my grandmother. She made sure I went to school and graduated with my high school diploma. We didn't have a lot of money, but I had the bare necessities I needed. She took me to church every Sunday, and I'm so grateful for that. Although my environment or community wasn't the safest place, she and my grandfather kept me as safe as they could. I wasn't allowed to sleep over at other people's houses, and I had a strict curfew. I give God praises often for allowing me to escape that place without a kid on my hip, addictions to drugs or alcohol, and still being alive. I didn't let my circumstances kill my dreams. I kept my goals in front of me and ignored the voices that told me I won't be nothing and will never amount to anything.

I didn't have any positive role models that looked like what I wanted to be or do. So, I started creating images in my head and began writing journals. I picked up books that would help me on my journey to getting out and becoming a better person. I prayed to God on a daily basis. I stayed away from people who didn't look like where I wanted to go in life. One thing for sure and still relevant today is that I've never been a follower and I believe that has kept me out of a lot of bad situations. Don't get me wrong, I did make some mistakes and bad choices along the way. In fact, some that could have cost me my life. But God had a plan for me since before I was born. For every wrong turn I made, He paved a right one. One of my favorite scriptures in the bible is: "For I know the plans I have for you, declares the Lord, plans to prosper you and not to harm you, plans to give you hope and a future" (Jeremiah 29:11).

I didn't discover these beautiful words until much later, but I see why as I now look back, that I had to have a mother who didn't protect me and a father who didn't care. God's love for me is unconditional. We humans have many flaws. We are not perfect. Christ died for our sins so that we can forgive and extend that same forgiveness to someone else. I didn't have hope before, but when I read that scripture, it set my soul on fire and I knew that without a doubt, my life would get better and I had a future that was already secured in God.

Lesson Learned

Indeed, my life did change when God sent my husband of 18 years plus into my life. At one time, I didn't think someone other than my grandparents was capable of loving me. Why would they? I came with a lot of baggage, a lot of doubt and had really bad low self-esteem. I felt as if I was in between a burning shade and a fading light. I was so broken, but God will take what is broken and use it for His glory. We met at a grocery store that I took three city buses one way to get to. I knew from the very beginning, that man was going to be my husband and the father to our children. He was unlike any man I had ever met and from a small town outside of Lafayette, LA. We married three years after meeting each other and moved from Louisiana to Dallas, Texas.

We settled in and tried to start a family of our own. That was one of the hardest and most challenging journeys of my life. For some time, my womb was barren. I thought getting pregnant would come easy for me since God knew that I would be a better mother to my kids and because my mother had no problem with childbearing. I didn't realize at the time that, before becoming the mother God called me to be, I had to do something that would require some maturity on my part. I had to ask God for forgiveness and then extend that same forgiveness to my mother. I believe that God wouldn't remove the blemish until I stopped nursing the resentments I had towards my mother. Sometimes, we can get stuck there too. Forever the kid, the "woe is me" victim mentality, and have not in the realm of love.

Well, what I have learned through my own observations looking back over the years, is that my mother did the best she knew how to do under the circumstances. History repeats itself, so they say. I know she didn't have a close, loving relationship with her own mother. Her mother and father divorced when she was just a young girl. I often wonder if my mother is the product of her own childhood too. Was she a victim of abuse? Has she ever thought about giving up on life? It's a conversation to date we've never had. I have learned to forgive my mother just as God forgave me for the mistakes that I have made.

"Bear with each other and forgive one another if any of you has a grievance against someone. Forgive as the Lord forgave you." Colossians 3:13

It's in the word of God that in return, we forgive others and offer grace as we have been shown grace. It can be one of the hardest things to do, especially when the hurt and pain that others caused us is absolute and great. But the pain of living with anguish and not being able to forgive, can rotten your soul and consume you. Forgiving my mother doesn't mean I'm saying what she did was okay, I'm just releasing her to God and letting go of its hold on me. I knew that forgiving my mother was the biggest step to healing my life and my womb. It was now six years into our marriage and there was still no baby. I didn't give up and wasn't giving up no time soon. We were young and anxious and ready to be new parents. We visited an infertility specialist and soon began treatment for IVF (in vitro fertilization). After the removal of a cyst (the size of a large lemon) and two rounds of IVF treatments later, we welcomed a set of twins (boy and girl) and we couldn't be any happier. But God wasn't done with me yet. As I was still being obedient to seeking forgiveness for my mother, healing was still happening and I didn't even know it. A year later, we found out we were with child again, this time without any infertility treatments. Won't He Do It?

Now that I'm older with three children of my own, I feel even more empathy towards her because mothering is not an easy job. I have forgiven myself and my mother for the pain we've both endured; from the deepest of wounds, that were carved out over many years. I believe that one day, I will be telling the story of how my mother and I reconciled our differences. I hate the idea of a sad ending. My hope is that circumstances will change to allow for a healthy and functional relationship in the future; but until then, I'm releasing any attachment to the outcome to create space for me to remain at peace, regardless of how the unknown unfolds. For now, I have the right to close the door in order to protect myself and my heart.

I will not allow history to repeat itself with my children and me. The cycle has been broken for generations to come. My love for my kids is one I cannot explain. They will never have to wonder about my love or their father's love for that matter. My job as their mother is to love and protect them. To help shape and mold them. To be their safe place. They know that they are cared for and loved unconditionally.

In conclusion, I will give you five lessons that I've learned on my beautiful journey that's leading to my beautiful destination.

1. I Had To Learn To Love Myself First

Practicing self-care is essential to maintaining a healthy relationship with yourself. It builds confidence, self-esteem and can increase true happiness over time. In the last few years, I've been very intentional about this practice because the former me was not a top priority in my own life. I showed up for everyone else but me. It wasn't until I hit rock bottom that I was able to stand on a solid foundation and rebuild my life with the confidence of God's unconditional love.

2. Learn To Love Others Where They Are

I was very hard on myself when it came to being kind to me. I didn't know how to do that or better yet, I didn't know how to accept that kind of love because I was so used to being mistreated by others. Don't take it personally when they push your love away. Not everyone is accepting of love that's pure and true. It's not something they're used to, and you can't force it on them. In the same way, I can't force my love on my mother. My hope is that one day, she'll see me for who I am; her daughter, a daughter that just wants to love her like she's never been loved before.

3. Forgive

The highest form of love you can give yourself and others is the gift of forgiveness. It releases you from pain and bitterness. I had to make a choice: will I dwell on the hurt and pain, or will I move on and make peace. Forgiveness has made ways for many open doors and has allowed me to see the plan God has for my life.

4. Parenting Doesn't Come With A Hand Book

It didn't for my mother and surely not for me. As a mother, I understand the sacrifices that come with parenting and making the best decision under the circumstances. It's a given that I will make mistakes as a parent because I'm not perfect. I will say, "Yes" when I should have said, "No," and I will say, "No" when I should have said, "Maybe." Just as God's grace is sufficient enough for me, so as it is for my mother. We both have God's grace, and because of that, we will rest in His power.

5. Let It Go

It's okay to unlearn things you thought you had to hold on to forever. If it no longer serves its purpose...let it go! I have learned there's power in transformation. Don't be afraid to let God transform you. You may miss out on who you could have been.

Latannia Locks

Latannia Locks, is a native of New Orleans, Louisiana and currently resides in Dallas, Texas along with the love of her life, husband, and best friend Kevin, 3 beautifully amazing children, & the star of their family, Rocky, their pet Boxer. She and her family are members of Oak Cliff Bible Fellowship and under the direct leadership of Dr. Tony Evans.

Latannia is a blogger, writer, author, and professional hairstylist who has dedicated her life to making women look and feel beautiful from the inside out. As a result of her own personal love for hair, she was featured in Modern Salon Magazine's December 2017 issue and deemed as one of their "Healthy Hairdressers" in the online publication November 2017.

Latannia has heart for community partnerships and has dedicated her personal time & services to various shelters which cater to both women & children who have been impacted by Domestic Abuse. Through her advocacy, she has been a guest speaker at events to promote social awareness and attacking the stigma of Domestic Violence. In her spare time, Latannia loves the great outdoors, spending time with family, reading, writing, and running. To connect with Latannia for future partnerships, speaking engagements, or hair services, reach out to her @ *llatannia@ gmail.com.*

Chapter 10

I Found My Treasure in the Darkness
Kelly Guyton

"I will give you hidden treasures, riches stored in secret places, so that you may know that I am the Lord, the God of Israel, who summons you by name." Isaiah 45:3

Life is a series of journeys we all will face. You will live & love & experience loss before your life is over. Losing some things will help you appreciate what you still have. It is the bitter taste of poverty that makes prosperity so sweet. How can you celebrate victory if you have never faced defeat? I am now on my 41st journey, and I can honestly say that I have experienced the good, the bad, and the ugly during my series of journeys. I am still here and standing only by the grace of God.

I can remember one of my journeys just like it was yesterday. This journey started in June of 2002. I was coming out of another journey where I was ending a very horrible and painful relationship that I should never have been in. A broken 25-year-old young lady whose heart felt as if it had been shattered into a thousand pieces. At the time, I was working two jobs; I was a licensed cosmetologist doing hair and working at a call center for this phone company. I remember going to work and seeing this young, tall guy sitting in the seat I usually sit in. Even though we didn't have assigned seats, everybody on my team knew this was my favorite seat. I became furious, so I walked up to him and I let him have it. The words that I spoke to him that day were not so kind. In fact, they were very ugly and included a few bad words. I ended with, "And tomorrow, you better not be in my seat!" He calmly and politely waited until I finished and he stated, "We don't have assigned seats, so you're welcome to sit in the seat I normally sit in." I was not happy about it, but I did just that.

The next day, I returned to work. In my mind, as I am walking in, all I could think was, "He better not be in my seat again." I get there, and there he was once again, in my seat! I was furious and I began to use those unkind and very ugly choice words and ended it with, "This is your final warning! Tomorrow, you better not be in my seat!" Again, he calmly and politely waited until I finished and he stated, "We don't have assigned seats, so you're welcome to sit in the seat I normally sit in." I'm now thinking in my mind, "What in the world is wrong with this dude?" He must be crazy! I didn't sit in his seat this time. I sat in another seat because, in my mind, I was thinking, "He can't tell me where to sit!" The next day I'm returning to work; I'm ready again. I'm thinking in my head, "He better not be in my seat today because I warned him." I get to work, and he was not in my favorite seat.

I was so happy I had my seat back. I start to prepare for the start of my shift, and I feel someone tap me on my shoulder. I turn around and it's him. The guy that kept sitting in my seat. He politely says, "Hello, how are you today?" If looks could kill, the look I gave him would have killed him. He stood there with a warm smile on his face. In a very rude tone, I said, "I'm doing just fine now that I have my seat back." He said, "Can I ask you a question?" I'm thinking, "What is wrong with this guy?" I then start to give him a look like, "You are really pushing it." I replied, "Yes! Yes! Yes! What is your question?" Calmly he asked, "Why does such a beautiful young lady, let such ugly words come out of her mouth?" That question caught me off guard and I couldn't say anything. He continued to say, "You are such a beautiful young lady. You should think about the things you say and do before you do it." He continued, "Please stop acting the way you do; loud, angry, always ready to fight." I couldn't say anything because he was right.

I was a broken young lady, but his calming voice was calming the raging storm that was going on inside of me. He stirred up my mind and his words were tugging at the little bit of heart that was still left. I started thinking, "Maybe I do need to change." He handed me his number and told me his name. As he walked away, he said, "You can call me sometimes if you just need someone to talk to." I was speechless. A couple of days passed and I was dealing with my hurt. I ran across his number, so I called him. From that day on, and for the next 4 years, we began to build a friendship bond that was unbreakable. Like most friendships, we had our ups and downs, smiles and frowns, good days & bad days, but our bond became stronger through all of our trials and tribulations. Being the young lady that was once so broken, I felt that God was using him to put my heart back together piece by piece with the love he was showing me through his encouragement and uplifting words. We made a promise to each other that we would never give up on each other and we would always be there for each other.

As the days went by, I was happy. I had joy, and my heart was mending as I was enjoying the previous journey I was on. I was thanking God for healing me and giving me a better life and for finally giving me a man that truly saw my worth. Now our friendship turned into a relationship. I was in a relationship with my best friend. My life was on track. I was in the process of building the perfect life with this man. We both loved God, we loved each other, I learned who he was and he learned who I was. It was perfect. I began to plan my life with him because I believed and was pretty sure we would end up taking it to the next step. I just knew that this would be the end of my hurt & pain. But what do you know? Life happened and something went wrong in the relationship and we broke up in November of 2005. A part of my heart shattered again. The breakup lasted for 30 days. I thought it was the longest 30 days that I had ever lived.

All this time, I had been thanking God and rejoicing, but I hadn't taken time to ask God what were the plans that He had for my life. We ended up working things out because it just seemed that we couldn't see living our lives without each other. Back at it again, enjoying life. The piece of my heart that was broken was now mended again. I was back on track in my happy relationship. Since we were broken up during the holidays and it was getting close to my birthday in March, he made a promise to me that he was going to make up for the lost time. Monday, March 13th 2006, came and it was my birthday. He had the whole evening planned out. He came over and my first surprise was a large chocolate chip cookie with a dolphin jumping out of the ocean. He gave me beautiful roses along with some pink and white Jordan shoes. He also gave me a little teddy bear that was holding his initial and we went out to eat at my favorite spot, The Cheesecake Factory. Our last stop after some good food was bowling. We loved to bowl and he was so competitive that he said, "If you beat me tonight in bowling, I will buy you anything that you want." I was excited and I just knew I was going to win, but I didn't... I lost.

As we were ending the night talking, I remember him saying that we have gone through good and bad times with each other and that he wanted to spend the rest of his life with me. He then kneeled down on his knee and said, "If I ask you tonight to marry me would you?" I said, "Yes, of course I would." He said, "Kelly, I have big plans for you this weekend. Be ready. Make sure you pack something nice to wear." My mind was racing and I was so excited. He just did a rehearsal proposal, so it must be the big proposal in front of all his friends. We had a weekend planned at the coast with some of our friends. He was going to do some deep sea fishing with the guys and the ladies were going to hang out. Everything was coming together. My plans were coming together. We had once talked about moving to Virginia if we ever decided to get married and since he had just asked that question, I knew the move would be next.

The next two days, I was running around getting stuff prepared for our weekend trip. On the Wednesday before we were scheduled to leave, he came over to see me before going to his part-time night job. Some things were bothering him. I remember encouraging him and uplifting him like he often did me. I let him know that the things he was dealing with, God was going to work them out because we serve an awesome God. Before leaving, he said, "I love you Kelly and I don't know what I would do without you." I told him, "No, I don't know what I would have done or what I would do without you." I continued, "I love you and

I'll see you later." On the following morning, March 16th 2006, I had my twin god-children over who had stayed the night with me so that I could take them to school. I remember turning on the news and it was saying there was a terrible accident on Palmer Lane in Austin, TX. I was like, "Oh No! That's our route. Let's leave early because we're going to have to take a different route."

I dropped the twins off and when I got to work and I received a call on my cell from my mom. She asked me when was the last time I had talked to my love. I said, "Last night before he went to work; and I tried to call him while he was at work, but I guess they were really busy because he never called back." I immediately begin to feel sick to my stomach. I tried calling him several times, no answer. I left work because I wasn't feeling well at all. I went to his house and his car was not there but his brother was. I asked him where he was and he said, "I thought he was with you Kelly on a trip." I was like, "No, that is not until the weekend." We began to call his friends and we rode around looking for him. Where was he? We got back to his house and I see my whole family standing in his yard. My dad, mom, aunt, brother and my best friend. I rush to my mom and said, "What happened?" She said, "He's gone." I screamed, "Gone where?" She said, "He passed away in a car accident." I fell to the ground and begin screaming, "NO! NO! NO! It wasn't him! It wasn't him! Please God! NO, don't do this to me! Please NO God!"

The last 4 years of my life with him were flashing in my head. My plans and my life had just changed that fast. My heart felt as if it was ripped out of my chest, thrown on the ground and shattered into thousands of pieces that day. As I go to the accident location where it occurred, and I see all the damage and stuff laying around, I stopped living on the inside. I felt empty and dead at that moment. I had so many plans. Now, everything was changed. How could I go on with my life when the person that I was planning to spend the rest of my life with had passed away? I felt there was nothing left here on this earth for me. I became angry with God because there were so many unanswered questions. How could God allow this to happen? How could God bring someone into my life that was helping me to heal my broken heart from previous hurt, now take him? Not only was I broken again, I was devastated and no longer wanting to live.

My days were now beginning to seem so much longer. I was just going through the motions. I might have been smiling on the outside but no one knew on the inside how I was really feeling. I was so broken, lonely, angry and empty. I went to the doctor and was told that I was depressed. The doctor wanted to prescribe me depression medication and some type of sleeping pills. That was not an option for me. I already felt that I was walking around like a zombie. My thought process was that the medication would only make things worse. I turned down counseling because I just didn't think that it would help me. Even though I was angry with God, confused and still had a lot of questions, I never stopped going to church. I was still drawn to the church.

Then the time came where I kept getting this feeling that I needed to relocate to Odessa, Texas but couldn't understand why. This is the place where my love was from. A place that he said he would never go back to. It was not easy for some of my family to accept, but I knew it had to be God because I felt at peace with the move. In May of 2006, I relocated to start a new life. I had hoped that something good would come out of this relocation, but all hope in anything good happening had been lost. In my mind, I'm saying, "Okay God, what is in store for my life now?" I was hurt, broken, empty, angry and lonely. I was now in a new place with no blood family or friends; but within me, I felt that this was something that I needed to do. I left the big city of Austin, Texas at a time I was feeling my lowest. I felt like I had nothing to live for. I was broken, lonely, angry and empty still wondering why this had happened to me. I was beating myself up and began to feel that maybe this was God's punishment for all the wrong that I have done in my life and for not always being obedient to his word. The devil was on his job day in and day out putting things in my mind that kept me feeling like I was in a black hole and couldn't climb out. In my mind, I didn't think anyone would or could understand me but there was one place that I knew I needed to be and that was church. I joined a church that his family and friends served at. I was isolated from everything and everyone that I was familiar with and I was no longer in my comfort zone.

The first year in my new location was pretty rough for me. I didn't too much care for the job I had. I wanted to pack up several times and return to my comfort zone but that same feeling that I would get when it was time for me to move here, kept coming up and making me feel as if I needed to stay. The second year came around and I began to make new friends and I became involved in the church. I also got a new job at the cable company that I enjoyed because not only was it a good job, but my coworkers were loving and very welcoming. I started to feel better. I wasn't 100%, but I started to feel like there was a purpose for me to live. God had a plan and I had no idea at the time, but I eventually became a teacher to the teenage class at church. When I was asked, the first thing that came to my mind was, "How can I teach or help these teenagers when I'm hurting myself?" At the time, I didn't even want to live so how would I be able to help a teenager who came to me saying that they didn't want to live anymore? My favorite line was, "I Can't Do This." When the thought of, "I Can't Do This" would come to my mind, I could hear a soft peaceful voice saying, "You Can Do This." So my scripture for the class became, "I can do all things through Christ who strengthens me" (Philippians 4:13).

That was perfect because not only was it going to help me, it was going to help those teenagers. In the midst of my pain, I had become a leader so I had to study my Word more than I had ever studied before. I had to have a lesson prepared for the class every week. I was building a rapport with them. The class was starting to open up to me and trusted me with things they had done and weren't proud of. They shared their feelings which were similar to my own so when I would encourage and uplift them, I was encouraging and uplifting me too. Now, as I was praying for God to heal and strengthen them, my prayers would be for God to do the same for me. I didn't understand what God was doing. One day when I was studying, I saw this scripture: "For my thoughts are not your thoughts neither are your ways my ways, declares the Lord" (Isaiah 55:8).

I knew during the good times and the bad times, I would never know or understand what God was thinking or doing but He wanted me to trust Him and have faith. My heart was slowly being healed through every lesson that I taught, every teenager in class that I gave encouraging and uplifting words to, every prayer that I prayed and every tear that I shed. Then, I realized it wasn't me. It was God using me to not only heal me, but to help heal others.

It was in my isolation from everyone and everything that was familiar to me that I learned how awesome God was. It took for me to be in a very uncomfortable place to start building a strong relationship with God. My Father and Mother raised me in church and they taught me about God. I often heard people tell testimonies about how great

God was and all the wonderful things He had done. How He brought them through hard times and how He brought them out of certain situations. It was now my time to experience what I had heard about for so many years. I was now in need of my mind, my heart, my soul being healed. God was doing just that by surrounding me with love and prayers. My relationship with God was going to a whole different level. The more I poured into those teenagers, the more God poured into me. I was now climbing out of that deep dark hole that was filled with hurt, depression, loneliness and suicidal thoughts. He was teaching me and preparing me for everything He had promised me. There was a purpose and a plan for me and everyone in this life. The hurt that I endured of losing someone that was very dear to me and who meant the world to me was a hurt that almost caused me on the inside to give up, quit and throw in the towel. I had lost all hope, but it was God's grace and tender mercy that kept me and covered me in the midst of such heartache and pain during one of my darkest and hardest journeys in life. I am a woman who experienced great loss and pain, but I remained loyal and faithful. By doing that, I found strength in God. "And we know that all things work together for good to those who love God, to those who are the called according to his purpose" (Romans 8:28). God has too much for me to do to waste any more time! I had to GET UP and climb out of that dark hole. It was in the darkness when I found my treasure (GOD). "For God, who said, "Let there be light in the darkness, has made the light shine in our hearts so we could know the glory of God that is seen in the face of Jesus Christ" (2 Corinthians 4:6).

I opened my heart to God and his light began to shine in the dark places inside of me so that I could start living again. What good is life without living? I shall live and until my dying day comes, I will continue to walk by faith and not by sight. I will pray that God places a song in my heart each morning that I open my eyes. I am still here and it's by the grace of God. This is not the end of my story. God is still writing my story and this is only part of it. To Be Continued…

Reflection & Lessons Learned:

Everyone handles loss differently. Sometimes, we turn to any and everything instead of turning to God. We turn to alcohol, drugs, pornography, religion, relationships, hobbies, television, social media, work etc. Not one of these things can or will satisfy us. There is only one who can satisfy us and that is God. No matter what obstacles, trials or tribulations we encounter on our journey of the loss of a loved one, always fully rely on God. I once heard a minister say, "Having a relationship with God gives you 7 Benefits":

1. **A HEAVENLY FATHER**

2. **A LIFETIME OF FORGIVENESS**

3. **A SATISFIED SOUL**

4. **A FOREVER FAMILY**

5. **A STRENGTHENING SPIRIT**

6. **A MEANINGFUL MISSION**

7. **A HEAVENLY HOME**

"The steadfast love of God never ceases his mercies never come to an end; they are new every morning; great is your faithfulness." Lamentations 3:22

Kelly Guyton

Kelly Guyton has been deemed a methodical leader with proven success in exhibiting core competencies and values to drive organizational results. She has an insurmountable track record in collaboration to build sustainable partnerships. Kelly has a broad range of professional training as a licensed cosmetologist and has used this platform as a means to minister and encourage women to live their best life.

Kelly is a member of PromiseLand Church, Lockhart, Texas under the leadership of her Pastor, Mike Hollifield. Having a heart for outreach, Kelly serves as a member of the Hospitality Team where she welcomes both members and guests to enjoy a life changing experience. Prior to, Kelly served as Ministry Leader for Singles and Youth at Living Vision Ministries in Odessa, Texas under the leadership of Pastor Elder James Porter.

A native of Lockhart, Texas, Kelly attributes her parents, Ira & Jacalyn Guyton for inspiring her to live a life for Christ & pursue obtaining her degree as she's currently scheduled to graduate from Odessa College with a degree in Business Administration. In her spare time, Kelly likes to read, travel, and journal. For speaking engagements, reach out to Kelly at *kellyguyton13@gmail.com*.

Chapter 11

Finding The Strength In Me

Kameron Jones-Marzette

"I can do all things through Christ who strengthens me."
Philippians 4:13

When I was asked to write a chapter in the Love, Life, and Lessons Learned anthology, I honestly didn't have a clue about what I would write about. Just recently coming off of the success of another anthology that I co-authored, I was truly fresh out of ideas. I prayed and soul searched about a topic that I could write about. I considered a few ideas, but being an author requires a great deal of vulnerability and courage. It can be scary sharing intimate details of your life. My hesitation led me to really think about my life. I asked myself, "What I could share that best embodies the three words love, life, and lessons?" I pondered and procrastinated with this for several weeks, but ironically I ended up discovering that the answer was right in front of me. My vision then became clear and that is how this chapter came to be.

To begin, I have been a teacher for over half of my life. Being a teacher defines who I am and what I am about. It's something that I love. So, it only made sense to me that I would write about my experiences as a teacher. Since I can remember, education has always been a priority to me. I understand the importance and value of knowledge. Education equips you with knowledge, and when you have knowledge, you become empowered. I come from a family that values education and hard work. As a result, I recognized at an early age that mediocrity just was not an option in my life. This is not to say that I have excelled in everything that I've attempted when it comes to academics. However, one thing that I've always been very adept of is where my strengths and weaknesses lie.

For many years, I always believed that math was my area of weakness. I can still remember from when I was in elementary school, having that anxious feeling when it was my turn to go to the board to solve a problem. I always acted confident on the outside, but on the inside, my stomach would be in knots. Basically, I felt that my success in this subject was hit or miss. It really just depended on what concept we were working on at the time. When I solved the equations perfectly, I felt good. But when I didn't, I felt ashamed and more like a failure. The type of the instruction at my school at the time really didn't do much to address those feelings of inadequacy. It was a sort of sink or swim mentality, either you got it or you didn't. As a kid, I obviously didn't know a lot about teaching and learning, but what I did know is that having a lack of understanding was a feeling that I didn't like having. Decades later, I don't believe that math was actually a weakness for me. Math did seem to pose more challenges for me, but I am sure that if I had been given more encouragement or differentiated instruction, I might not have gone through elementary school feeling nervous every time I opened a math book. We tend to shy away from things that make us uncomfortable, but what I needed to know from my teachers at the time was that we all don't learn the same.

Now that I am an educator myself, I have a better understanding of how instruction works. Teachers of my childhood era taught according to the expectations of education during that time period. Students listened, the teacher taught, and we showed our mastery of content through paper and pencil tasks. While this probably suited a generalized population of students, it simply didn't do much for those who may have needed a challenge, or those who needed additional reinforcement. Education for the masses actually doesn't help the masses learn better. Fortunately for me, I had enough experiences and support at home to compensate for the shortcomings that methodical education offered. I also would be remiss to discount my inner drive to succeed. This drive definitely surpassed any feelings that I may have had of ever giving up. So throughout my primary and secondary education, I worked hard, asked questions, sought out resources, shined despite my personal fear of failure.

I successfully navigated my way through grade school and high school. I was ready for college. I grappled with what I would study in college. My perceived deficiencies in math made me steer away from programs in math/science related fields. In a discussion about this with my dad, I remember what he told me. He said, "One thing is for sure, there is always a need for teachers, so you'll always have a job!" Getting a job after college was always at the forefront of my thoughts, but I also knew that it had to be something that I would also enjoy doing. I declared my major in education. College was demanding, but I actually breezed my way through my pre-requisite and core classes. Throughout my 4 years in college, I would tell people that I wanted to become a teacher to make a difference in the lives of children. In all actuality, I didn't even really know what that truly meant. My coursework gradually started to help me construct a framework for the needs of students and give me textbook strategies for instruction. I was given many opportunities to observe classroom teaching too, which gave me some ideas about what I would and wouldn't want to do when I became a teacher. The closer that I got to the end of my program, I knew my vision of how I wanted my classroom environment to be. I wanted to have a classroom that was structured yet fun, challenging yet encouraging. What I didn't know was how I was going to do that, but at least I had an idea in my head. What was clear to me was that no matter what, I wanted to be a good teacher in whatever context that defined. With much trial and error, I can safely say that I've given my best effort at doing that.

My career journey has been met with a few bumps along the way. I loosely characterize it with a plethora of adjectives: Exciting and frustrating; fun and challenging; confusing and exhilarating; and definitely exhausting! All of these adjectives and many more in between illustrate the highs and lows of my career.

I got my first inkling of what being a full-time teacher was all about during my student teaching placement. My first placement was in a district in which the demographics were diverse racially and economically. I went in with rose-colored glasses on so to speak. The teacher was very organized and knowledgeable and I enjoyed watching her interact with the students. What I liked most was that the kids seemed to truly enjoy being in her class. I coasted through that placement and I was energized to start the next one. This time, I was placed in a district in which the demographics were very different. The student population was primarily African-American and in many ways, the students were considered to be at-risk. This experience was very new to me. Although my education certainly had some shortcomings, I had actually attended private schools all of my childhood and teenage years. That's not to imply that private schooling is better, just different. Public education was a new arena for me, especially one with academic and behavioral challenges.

Nonetheless, this experience was good for me. I was able to see a wide range of learning styles and strategies. My biggest take away early in my career was that despite pre-conceived stereotypes, all children come to school ready to learn. It is our responsibility as educators to ensure that their experiences are authentic, worthwhile, and beneficial. While student teaching, I was offered a full-time teaching position. I was so grateful to be given the opportunity to have my first full-time job that I didn't even consider how hard it would actually be. Other than student teaching, I had very little hands on preparation for working with students. This left me with a great deal of textbook knowledge, but no real experience in the classroom. Nevertheless, I was eager to embark on the newest chapter of my life. I researched all of the cool activities and lessons to use with my class. I referred back to my class notes from undergrad. I knew the district had a set curriculum, but I wasn't worried about that. I was more concerned about doing the fun stuff. In my mind, I wanted to make learning pleasurable so that the kids would like me and not get bored. I figured I could teach what the kids needed to know and still do all the cutesy, enjoyable activities with *every* lesson. I quickly got a reality check.

My very first class of students as a full-time teacher was taxing, to say the least. I started in January, which was right after the long holiday break and in the middle of the school year. The kids came back kind of sluggish and had all but forgotten my quick introduction the month before. Naively, I had envisioned myself stepping into my new assignment, implementing all of my fresh ideas, and having the students love everything about me. Needless to say, that was not the case. I had my work cut out for me! The class already had a routine and relationship with the previous teacher that they actually did love. Starting with day one, I struggled just to get through the lessons and deal with discipline problems. The kids could sense my inexperience and they took advantage of that. I really was learning everything on the job with very little preparation. I remember how I would often observe other teachers with their classes or eavesdrop on some of their lessons while passing by in the hallway. They all seemed to have it all together and they seemed to do it with such ease. Feeling beat up, I would go home feeling tired and discouraged every evening after school. I sometimes even doubted if I had even chosen the right career. God stayed in my ear though, telling me to persevere. While my fellow co-workers were cordial, they weren't jumping at the chance to help me, the new girl. In retrospect, I definitely see why they didn't. Teaching demands a great deal of time and energy. It's often difficult to accomplish all of the tasks that you are expected to do, let alone additional things that you don't have to do. As a veteran teacher now, I think differently. I feel more compelled to help teachers or staff members that I see struggling. I know from experience, it's a terrible feeling to know that you're failing, but have no one to pull you up.

As time progressed, with much prayer and resilience, I did finally make a connection with a small group of teachers professionally and socially. It's important to feel like you are a part of a team, especially when a common goal is shared. However, each day when I'd walk into my classroom and close the door, I realized that no matter how much support and kindness that I was shown, it really was just the kids and me. I had no other choice than to make the best of my situation and teach those kids the best way that I knew how.

I decided to take the initiative and turn my situation around. First, I started by carefully planning out each day the night before. I tried to anticipate things that could potentially go wrong with each lesson so that I could have an alternate plan in mind. Next, I tried out different teaching strategies, and I reached out to other teachers when I needed help or advice. At first, I was apprehensive about asking questions, but I had to put my fears aside and start partnering up with my co-workers. This was when I began to understand what the business of teaching was all about. All of the stress that I was feeling started to lessen when I stopped feeling sorry for myself and I started collaborating. No class or textbook could have given me what I needed to succeed that year. Then, a couple of months into my new career, things finally began to turn around. It seemed as if overnight the kids started changing. We had some minor issues here and there, but for the most part, our days went smoothly. I also started to observe that the students were behaving better and they were a lot more focused on their lessons. I felt excited when I would see their smiling faces walk through the door, eager to start their day. I got to know my students' likes and dislikes, learning preferences, and personalities. Not only was I building relationships with my co-workers, but I was also building relationships with my students. It took me some time to truly make this connection, but when children know that you value them, they begin to feel more confident. Then, they'll trust you on a more personal level. Once you have their trust, they'll try to make every effort to meet your expectations.

Consequently, my own confidence was increasing too. My principal expressed that she was pleased with my work and the progress that I was making with my students. Overall, life was good for me and I was proud that I was resourceful enough to make it through that stressful time. Even though I was a first year teacher, I never let my lack of experience keep me from doing my best. I was determined to not give up on myself or those kids that year. I worked hard and before I knew it, those five months had flown by. Just when I had started to catch my breath, the school year was over.

I thoroughly enjoyed my summer after that school year. It was a good feeling knowing that I had a full-time job to return to and a little bit of experience under my belt. That anxiousness that I had initially had all but gone away. However, the feeling of euphoria quickly came to an end. Midway through the summer, I received a termination letter that put a damper on everything. Positions were being cut in the district and because I was a new hire, my job was one of the first to go. My safe world suddenly became the unknown. I still lived at home so some of the usual responsibilities like a mortgage and household bills weren't as much of a concern then. Even though I had a cushion, I liked my job and I still wanted to work! Shortly after the letter, I received a phone call from the personnel director. He informed me that he possibly had another position for me in the district. Of course, that also meant that it would be at a different school. True to his word, a couple of weeks before the new school year started, I was placed in the district at another school. I felt such a relief! Another bonus about the new school was that it was actually closer to my house. The teacher that was my teammate at the time was awesome. She was helpful in every way and she was always willing to give advice when I needed it. In fact, the staff as a whole at this school was very friendly. Everyone appeared vested in the students and the success of the school. I made many lifelong friends that I still communicate with to this day. Probably the best part about this new transition for me, however, was that I felt like I was a part of a community. They valued opinions, supported ideas, and gave teachers some flexibility to be creative. The culture of a school can be extremely important. It often defines the success or failure of the school. I felt as though the children saw the staff as a united front committed to improving their educational experience.

Year after year, I continued to gain more knowledge and confidence. I started to really hone my craft. Ironically, even though I had more experience, I still don't think that I had everything together. I was pretty good with discipline and the students responded well to me. But it seemed as though the list of needs for the children were growing and becoming more extreme. Behaviorally and academically the students just needed more and I was beginning to question if I was equipped to address their needs. I wanted to understand my students and figure out what worked with them. Graduate classes and professional development provided me with information that I thought I could readily apply in my classroom. However, I wasn't always successful at doing this. It's much easier to tell someone what or how to teach than actually being in the trenches and doing the work.

Teaching may look easy, but it's a craft that requires great skill and navigation. I often found myself resorting to teaching in the manner that I was accustomed to and that I found comfortable for me. Frustrated and disappointed in myself, I would go back to the basics using review and reinforcement techniques until I knew that the students got it. In order for me to feel like a success with these children, I wanted them to actually be a success. This meant that my students had to not only understand the content but also be able to apply what they learned. Merely being able to impart knowledge is not teaching. What I figured out was that in order to be great as an educator, I needed to come in every day dedicated, motivated, and committed to doing whatever it took to help my students learn. That also brought a realization that I was going to have to wear a variety of hats, and some days it wasn't going to be the teacher hat. Nowadays, it may be the counselor hat, the mediator hat, the confidant hat, the nurturer hat, the mentor hat, and possibly even the parent hat. Some days it may be all of those simultaneously because our roles are not so clearly defined anymore. Children need us for a variety of things for a variety of reasons. Schools can't provide everything for a child, but we certainly try to come very close to it. I have evolved to be what my students need me to be.

My childhood was full of meaningful experiences and support which helped me to achieve my goals. The reality is that larger populations of children just don't have those experiences. As I've come full circle in my career, I can say that I've loved, lived, and learned a tremendous amount along the way. Knowing the grave consequences of a lack of preparation for the demands of the 21st Century motivates me to continue to push children to work hard. As I near the end of the teaching chapter of my life, I look forward to making an impact in children's' lives in a different capacity. Success is bound only by the limits that you place upon yourself and I am discovering all that I have to offer. Helping students achieve is a charge that I haven't taken lightly. I would never want a child to have that same feeling of inadequacy that I had long ago in math class. I no longer want to just teach, I want to inspire.

5 Inspirational Lessons I've Learned Along the way with Guiding Scriptures:

1. Put GOD first in your life. Remember that He gave you a purpose in life and you are a unique and valuable being. Serve Him first and you will see how He will fulfill you and ultimately change your life. (Psalm 73:24)

2. Approach things in your life with confidence even when you're terrified on the inside. Once you believe that you can do it, no one can stop you. (Joshua 1:9)

3. Don't be derailed by failure or mistakes in your life. Failure can be the best lesson to help motivate you to come back stronger the next time. (Philippians 4:13)

4. Find your purpose and pursue it. Then, cultivate meaningful relationships that have purpose in your life. (Proverbs 13:20)

5. Work hard, serve, and be committed. Be authentic when interacting with others and stay true to yourself. Let your good deeds and service be an example of your character. (Galatians 5:13)

In closing, I would suggest for you to always remain passionate about what you choose to pursue and be an inspiration to others. Set the tone for peace, perseverance, and positivity. Your aura will begin to attract others who hold similar values. Lastly, be grateful for every opportunity and remember to show your gratitude through your words and actions.

Kameron Jones-Marzette

Kameron Jones-Marzette is an award winning, best-selling author, educator, and speaker from St. Louis, Missouri. She has over 28 years of classroom experience where she has spent the majority of her life pouring into the lives of children by providing a nurturing yet challenging learning environment. Kameron promotes 21st Century skills, and her goal is to motivate children to become lifelong learners and global thinkers.

Kameron is a strong proponent of education, women's empowerment, and community partnerships to serve the underserved. She has a diverse educational background having earned degrees in Elementary and Special Education, Educational Leadership, and Adult and Higher Education. Well on her way to completing her Master's Degree in Library and Information Sciences, she will utilize this platform for empowering children and encouraging them to make a positive difference in the lives of others.

Kameron is married to Terry Marzette Jr. and she is the proud mother of one daughter, Katelyn & Kardi B, an undeniably cute Yorkshire Terrier. Kameron attends The Gate Church under the leadership of Pastor Kyle Hubbard & Pastor Benji Varner. To partner with Kameron for future speaking engagements, contact her at *kamshopalot@aol.com.*

Chapter 12

Evolving from a Caterpillar to a Butterfly
Samaria Tago

"My grace is sufficient for you, for my power is made perfect in weakness." 2 Corinthians 12:9-11

I lost my dad in December 2009, two days before Christmas and 4 days before my birth-day. We buried him on Jan 2, 2010. Losing my dad was tough; I was a daddy's girl. He was my protector and model for what a man should be in my life. I remember lying in bed one night and I heard him call out to God and say, "Jesus Christ! Come get me. I'm ready." At that moment, it felt as if my head was spinning on my shoulders. The next morning, I sat by my dad's side and said, "Daddy did you ask God to come get you last night?" He said, "Baby, I did." He said, "I'm ready." I have been a man's man all my life; and right now, I'm flat on my back." I so desperately wanted to cry in front of him, but I had to push the tears back. I had to be strong for him and my mom. I thought my world was falling apart. I was in charge of all my mom and dad's medical decisions. Making the decision to go through with hospice, was the hardest. I felt as if I was saying it was okay too, for my dad to die. I truly felt guilty. My brother and I talked and agreed it was for the best. While I was losing my dad, a friend said, "Losing Dad is hard, but losing Mom is when it really hits home." In my mind I'm like, "Girl please, my dad and I were like buddies." We disagreed, cracked jokes, laughed, told stories and enjoyed sports together. We would even crack jokes on my mom. My dad charged me with the task of making sure my son completed college and making sure my mom was okay and taken care of. After losing my dad, I remember lying in bed asking God to send my life partner. I didn't want to experience losing another parent without that special someone by my side.

Fast forward to 2013, I was in a good place in life. I loved my new place and my son was at his college. I was in a good place mentally and emotionally. I had my vision board of things I wanted to accomplish. Oh boy, I was on a roll. December 2013 rolls around and I thought I met the person I had been praying for. Anything I was interested in, he had the same interest. Even more exciting was the fact that we shared the same interests, goals, dreams, and love for God. He had a great career as a civil servant. Mind you, he was supposed to put fires out not start them. Whenever we were out, he was a gentleman. We would see his coworkers out, and they would speak really well of him. We even would crave the same foods at the same time of day. He was complimentary and always wanted to see me. He even cried one day because he said no one has ever made him feel the way I did. When we went places, people would say how great we looked together. Whenever my mom was ill, he would help the nurses out at the hos-pital. One nurse even told me, "He's a keeper." He presented himself very well. About 4 months in, we were at dinner one day. He asked, "Do you ever offer to pay for dates?" I said, "Excuse me Sir?" My sister girl attitude starts to appear. I'm baffled at this point-confused. I said, "Hon-estly, I have never been asked that question whenever I'm dating; secondly, the nerve of you. What happened to pursuing someone you're interested in?" The conversation goes left at this point. Then the comparison starts. He said, "Well women I've dated, always offered to pay." I said, "I don't mind paying, but that's later down the line." That was the first of many signs to come. Have you ever been dating someone and their actions cause you to question yourself? That's exactly what happened to me. Instead of saying, "Hey, I like you but I think our beliefs are different when it comes to certain things." I just continued to carry on and look at it as a small misunderstanding. Have you ever known when you know you should have ended the rela-tionship with someone? If you're like me, you probably have. Honestly, I should have ended this relationship 6 months into our dating.

One day, he and I were coming back from dinner. I said, "Baby, I have a question. I don't mean any harm, but I notice that when I have things that need to go to the dumpster, you walk past them and never offer to take them for me." I asked, "Can you explain why? I thought it was the gentleman thing to do?" Oh my, that turned into the biggest argument ever! You would have thought I ask him to jump into the dumpster. I said, "Well, I raised my son always to help ladies out and if there is trash, take care of it for her." Oh boy, he told me that he is not a trash man but a civil servant and his mom told him to never take trash out for his lady or any other woman. That turned into a five day silent treatment. I would call and text, no response. On the 6th day, he appeared and said he was sorry but some of my actions reminded him of his ex. He goes on to say that during this time, God was dealing with him. My logical mind understands; but if we are in a relationship, don't you think it's ok to communicate that? From there, he started telling me that I don't understand God and that any other woman would appreciate that. If I told him that I was going to Target and he called and I was at Walmart, he would ac-cuse me of not being a woman of my word. If I cooked and told him dinner would be ready at 7:45; but because I worked, I didn't have it ready until 8pm, I was a liar and not a woman of my word. If we were going somewhere and we were scheduled to leave at 8pm and didn't leave until 8:10, that was a problem. You know how we women take extra time to make sure we are looking good and everything in the right place? Yanooo' how we do it, ladies. That was a prob-lem. Slowly, I started changing things about me and almost reporting my every move just to keep arguments at a minimum. I didn't realize how much of myself I was actually losing. I was always trying to accommodate and smooth things over, which is not the normal Sam. The Sam I know had a voice and that voice was slowly becoming more and more quiet.

Fast forward to December 2015. He and I were still together and had decided to work on things and make it work. I sat down and wrote out my goals of different things I wanted to accomplish for 2016. Made my vision board, devised exit and strategy plans. "A man's heart plans his course, but the Lord determines his steps" (Proverbs 16:9).

Little did I know what was awaiting me for January 2016. My life changed forever. My mom, the love of my life was called home. Her work here was done. She ran her course, she finished her race. She was my confidant, best friend, counselor, the person who knew every-thing about me and still loved me. She was the person who lit up when I walked into the room. The one who believed I could do anything. My voice of reason, nurturer, first playmate, first hug and kiss. Not to mention, two days later, I lost my job and the team I had built for a small business had dissipated by February 2016.

In a matter of days, the world I was accustomed to, no longer was. My new reality was: I was without my mom, job and now both of my parents. I thought at least one of them would live to see me happily married, accomplished and thriving in life. I tried so hard to make sure that was the case. What was interesting about my mom and dad were they died on the same day of the week (Wednesday) and I buried them in the same month. I guess that's what happens when you've been married 55 years. Through their marriage, I was able to witness the ups and downs of a relationship; as well as the staying power it takes to make it work. I learned re-lationships aren't about good feelings all the time, but more so, about commitment. It wasn't always sunshine, but they made a commitment to make it work. I was blessed to see "Till death do us part," lived out. I was trying to grasp the reality of my mom being gone, income, health insurance, stability and the security of being able to pay my bills as well as being able to take care of myself.

I felt vulnerable in so many ways. Losing my mom took the breath out of me. I could literally feel my heart aching. I was trying to deal with the reality of her being gone while trying to maintain a normal life, in a world that does not allow anyone to properly grieve. I was ex-pected to carry on like everything was A-OK! I was told, "WOW, your attitude sure has changed." "Why wouldn't it?" I wanted to ask. I was told, "You act as if you're the only one who lost a mother." You know I wanted to go straight for their throat, right? I said to myself, "Sam, you don't need any charges on you. Stay calm." The guy who I decided to make it work with walked out four hours after my mom took her last breathe. He said that he was calling my name while I was responding to someone about my mom and I disrespected him. He said that if he had just lost his mom, that would not get in the way of him answering me because that's just how important I am. Yea, right dude. I felt lost, alone, confused, misunderstood, vulnerable, afraid, depressed, angry at life, myself and at God; to be honest. I remember going places and feeling completely disconnected. I would be in mid-conversation and then, I'd zone out.

For a while, I felt I was in a twilight zone. Where my world was once colorful but was now, black and white. Nothing made sense. During this time, I learned who was for me and who wasn't. I learned you really never know who has your back until that dark moment in life comes. Everyone says they will ride with you until it's actually time. I learned not many can ride this journey with you if it isn't benefiting them. I've learned you need the kind of friends and family that will stand by your side when they really can't understand you at the moment, nor when you can't formulate the words to explain. It was a painful experience. I would ask God, "Why now?" "Why didn't you show me this before mom passed?" This is the time I needed those, who I thought had my back, the most. I had so many questions but very few answers. One song that resonated with my spirit was "DEAR GOD" by Smokie Norful. Many would say, "Sam, you have to get out and enjoy life." Enjoying life was very far-fetched at that moment for me, but I knew that was probably true. Honestly, I didn't have the money to get out and enjoy anything. The money I saved went towards funeral expenses.

So many questions raced through my mind: How will I make it without my mom? What are my next steps? What am I to do with my life? Who can I trust? Surviving became what felt like a minute to minute choice/struggle. I no longer wanted to write about goals, dreams or plans.

I said, "What's the point?" I felt as though I couldn't trust anyone or anything. I'll be to-tally honest; I got so low that I was going to commit suicide. At the moment, it seemed like it was the only answer to end all the pain, hurt and disappointment. It seemed the only option left. I said, "God I have done what you asked of me. I honored my parents, I taught my son to love and honor you. I have given when I didn't have it to give. Lord, it seems you have taken a lot and replaced very little." I would lie in bed and ask for God not to wake me up in the morn-ing. When I did wake up and see I was still here, I would be upset. It felt as though I was being awakened to be punished. All the cliché sayings were the last thing I wanted to hear. Little did I know, it was all a part of his His plan. It felt as though my emotional pain was too much for me to bear as well as those around me. By September 2016, I'd had enough.

I was in a roommate situation that left me holding the bag. Quite honestly, going into a roommate living arrangement was not the best idea. I needed time to grieve and come to grips with everything. Financially, I thought it was the best option but in the long run, it wasn't. Two weeks before September, rent was due. I was told by my then-roommate/best friend that they would be moving. Mind you, I was making 11 dollars an hour less than my normal salary, with 8 months left in the lease. I didn't have a rich husband, boyfriend or family members; but I had to figure it out. My family did what they could. I'm eternally grateful for them. My credit score that I worked hard to build was also on the rocks. Where I could once walk in and get anything needed, was no longer the case. Now I'm really asking God, how will I make it? Always remem-ber He has a ram in the bush.

My god-brother's engagement party was coming up. I didn't want to let him down, so I mustered up enough strength to attend. It was a beautiful event. Most of all, I was happy he found true love. My plan after the event was to go home and follow through with my plan of suicide. If not that night, for sure Monday morning. Let's just say God had other plans. After my god-brother proposed, we all gathered around to take pictures. I noticed a woman at the back of the room looking at me. I thought, "Why is she looking at me so intensely? And for what?" Fast forward to the end of the night. I went to the back of the room to find a place to sit down. I just needed some time to myself. So many thoughts were flooding my mind. Mostly about my mom and how I was ready to take my life that night.

As I'm sitting there, the lady joins one of my long-time buddies and me. He and I began to talk. He went on to say that he was sorry for missing my mom's funeral and I told him that I understood and that there were no hard feelings. So the lady that was watching us take pictures up front sat across from me. She said, "I'm sure you noticed me looking at you." I said, "Yes I did." She said, "You were standing up there, and you had a glow and white light around you." Mind you, I've never seen this lady before. Didn't know her at all. We began to talk. She starts talking and it's in the manner of my mom's voice and spirit. My eyes begin to well up with tears. She said, "Your mom told me to tell you she has been trying to get to you but you haven't had the right people around you." She continued with, "She told me to tell you she loves you! She told me to tell you to start back praying how she taught you and to always remember you have an angel on your left and right side at all times. Start calling on them, call on God and your ancestors." By this time, I'm totally messed up. She said, "Your mom said that plan you have for suicide, you need to cancel it. GOD has a bigger plan for you." She said, "One day, you're going to be a change agent for a lot of people." Honestly, that was so far from my mind. I was trying to figure out how to make it day to day. I thought, "Really God? A change agent?"

"For I know the plans I have for you," declares the LORD, "plans to prosper you and not harm you, plans to give you hope and a future." (Jeremiah 29:11)

I cried the entire car ride home. Under normal circumstances, that would not have hap-pened. When you're involved with someone who is emotionally abusive and with narcissistic traits, walking away isn't so easy. The emotional abuse I suffered in this relationship, I vowed not to let another woman go through this alone. This caused me to research emotional abuse and how it had affected me. What I learned was:

Emotional abuse is defined as: "any act including confinement, isolation, verbal assault, humili-ation, intimidation, infantilization, or any other treatment which may diminish the sense of identity, dignity, and self-worth."

I also learned, "Emotional abuse is also known as psychological abuse or as 'chronic verbal aggression' by researchers. People who suffer from emotional abuse tend to have very low self-esteem, show personality changes (such as becoming withdrawn) and may even become depressed, anxious or suicidal."

Most people feel if it isn't physical, it's not abuse. That's not true. Emotional abuse af-fects you in ways that aren't visible. It's psychological, it's subtle and hard to detect. It includes mind games, threats of walking away, ending the relationship or you're made to feel you aren't good enough. I'm sure there are hundreds if not thousands of silent victims out there. This was the hardest breakup I have ever experienced; much harder than my divorce. It felt like a part of my soul had been ripped apart. All along, I was thinking I was loving someone who had not been shown love or properly loved (well, that's what he told me). In any story, he was always the victim; from childhood to adult relationships. A few weeks after my mom was buried, he came back with tears and an apology. He said that he wanted to make this right and he knew this is what Mrs. Johnson (my mom) wanted. I said, "Wow, God heard my cry and answered my prayers." So I thought. I mean, why wouldn't I give it another try? We had 3 years of history. Although there were many red-flags along the way, I didn't want to be alone; especially after losing my mom. I didn't want to start over nor did I have the energy to. He took me to look for rings and we narrowed it down to one. With the threat of always slowing the relationship down, it was very conditional. He would pick me apart with everything I did until he found a reason why we couldn't move forward with engagement.

Rewind back to a few days before my mom died. We had an argument which turned physical. Let's just say I attended my mom's funeral with bruised arms and body. Not only was I sitting there trying to grasp the reality of my mom being gone, but I was also emotionally and now physically hurting. It was double the pain. I wanted to wear a sleeveless dress to my mom's funeral but instead, I wore a cardigan over my dress to hide the bruises. I dare not let my family and friends see what had happened. Fast forward, I had this grand idea for us to attend pre-marital counseling. We attended a few sessions and by the 3rd session, the counselor pulls me to the side and says, "You have a lot to look at with him. He's narcissistic." I was totally naive to what a narcissistic was. So, I did more research and found the following:

Narcissism is referred to as excessive or erotic interest in oneself and one's physical appearance. Other words to describe a narcissist is one who has vanity self-love, self-admiration, self-absorption, egotistical, extremely selfish.

Even after then, it took me months to end our relationship. I tried several times before, but always went back. However, this time, he let go as well with a bit more ease. I later found out that he had met a new supply. What I mean by new supply is, he had found someone to give him the things that I once gave him. Narcissists always need to be constantly fed with attention, praise, admiration and they want you to be under them 24 hours a day. When out in public they want all the attention on them. They are never wrong about anything, nor do they take confrontation well. They will find a way to turn it back on you. Even if they made you feel bad about something, you will be told it's your fault and you made them do it. When you first meet a narcissist, they will make you feel as if you're the best thing since sliced bread. That's what I learned is the "Love Phase." You are showered with compliments and adoration. You will feel as though this is your soul mate! After you have been wooed in, you will experience the "Devalue Stage." This is where your confidence, your self-esteem and the sense of who you are is cut down. It's the beginning of the control over you "Control Phase." It's slow and subtle. They may begin to say how they don't like your friends or family or maybe your personal appearance (which is something they loved before). You will start to see cracks in what you thought was the perfect partner. I'll say this, "Always trust your intuition."

Being involved with a Narc robs your soul. You will have low energy, you will question things about yourself that you never questioned before. Narcs do not show remorse for the im-posed hurt and will never admit to any wrongdoings that's with you or anyone else. I wanted to share this with you because I had no one around me to bring light that I was in an emotionally abusive or narcissistic relationship. I want you to know you're not alone and if you're feeling this, you're right. Look at the signs and pay close attention. I don't want you to suffer in silence nor feel ashamed. It's not your fault. It's not okay nor is it normal. Honestly, it took a lot to be this transparent. I remember writing in my journal on August 20, 2016 that one day, I would share my story to help someone else. I said, what the enemy tried to use to break me, God will use to reach thousands. I am glad to have shared my story & may God bless you richly. My goal is not to let another person suffer in silence.

Let me conclude by sharing 5 lessons learned:

1. Always pray and seek God even when it seems like your prayers are going unanswered. Seek your own relationship with our Father in Heaven.

2. Always trust your intuition. If it doesn't feel right to you, chances are, it's not.

3. Don't expect people to treat you like you have treated them. A friend once told me to always do what's right and right will follow me.

4. Don't always expect to be understood. Keep moving forward.

5. No matter how dark it gets, God has a purpose in the storm. Trust me, you will come out stronger.

Samaria Tago

Samaria Tago is an award winning leadership professional with a strong background in strategic thinking, marketing, and sales. Samaria has several years' experience as an image consultant and make-up artist with a huge love for making women feel their best by looking their best. She utilizes her professional experience and couples it with her personal passion to positively impact the lives of women she touches in hopes of them paying it forward.

Samaria is a residing member of The Potter's House under the leadership of Bishop T.D. & Mrs. Serita A. Jakes. Honing in to her spiritual gifts, Samaria has served in various ministries which make a deep impact to others through outreach as well as hospitality. Placing a deep emphasis on servant leadership, Samaria is dedicated to compounding both her passion and her purpose to continue serving women and children who have been victimized by all forms of domestic & emotional abuse.

Samaria attended Tarrant County College majoring in Business Management. She is the proud mother of an amazingly successful son, Jamal and her cute fur baby, Sapphire. For speaking engagements or community partnerships, Samaria can be reached at *stago2525@gmail.com*.

Chapter 13

Love is an Action
Ruby Belcher

"And now these three remain: faith, hope and love. But the greatest of these is love." 1 Corinthians 13:13

I believe love is an action. It's doing what you say you're going to do. Being present, being engaged. In return, that's how I show my love to you. By being present, being engaged, going all out, protecting you, and fighting for you. That's also how I would gauge your love for me. How present are you in my life? How have you kept your promises to me, how often have you called? Have you put as much or more effort (in my opinion) into me as I did you?

We have to take into account that everyone has their own love language, and they often love you according to their love language instead of yours. What I've learned is that most people don't understand nor do they know about the different love languages. God has provided many tools for us to obtain knowledge, whether it's through His word or other sources. But we are prone to busyness, selfishness, lack of effort, lack of knowledge or all of the above. We don't take the time to do our homework. What people fail to realize is it takes just as much or more effort to maintain a good healthy relationship as it takes to get up in the morning and make a living. We need to go after love, peace and harmony like we go after the mighty dollar!

A lot of people operate out of "I've got you now" syndrome which is saying, "I've done all my work to get you, now I shouldn't have to continue to work to show that I love you." But that is so far from the truth because it's an ongoing process of actions. Let me give you some examples from the book, *The 5 Love Languages* by Gary Chapman.

There are 5 different love languages:

- Words of Affirmation: Expressing affection through spoken affection, praise, or appreciation.

- Acts of Service: Actions, rather than words, are used to show love.

- Receiving Gifts: Gifting is symbolic of love and affection.

- Quality Time: Expressing affection with undivided, undistracted attention.

- Physical Touch: Having sex, holding hands, kissing.

Say your love language is words of affirmation. Yet, you're giving praise and showing affection and appreciation to a person whose main love language is quality time. Even if your heart is in the right place and you're really trying to please the other person, that person may not receive your efforts because you are not speaking "their" language. What they're in need of is time and your undivided attention. There's going to be conflict because you can't really tell a person how to be loved, or what they need in order to feel loved. But that's often how we tend to treat people in our lives. We treat people according to our own needs; out of our own love language. And then we wonder why we don't get the responses we are looking for.

I often wonder if that's how God feels. If I had to guess, I would say His ultimate love language is quality time. He wants to sit and spend time with us, wants our uninterrupted, undivided, intimate time. God loves to pour into us. "But when you pray, go into your room, close the door and pray to your Father, who is unseen. Then your Father, who sees what is done in secret, will reward you"(Matthew 6:6). This scripture clearly states that He wants some one on one time.

I've been married for 14 years to an introvert. He is content with going to work and coming home. He enjoys his time alone for long periods of time. He loves to just chill at home and would rather not go out (in my opinion). But me on the other hand, I love going out! Sometimes I spend 8 hours at a time just hanging out going place to place with my little sidekick, my 3-year-old daughter. She's my ride or die. My husband requires alone time to recharge, so I would on purpose give him at least 30 minutes or an hour to himself after he gets home from work, before I bring any important issues to him. But often he would sometimes need a little extra time to himself depending on his day at work. He would just sit in the room for hours at a time watching television or playing Nintendo. At first, it was ok; but after a while, I started to feel alienated.

Now, I described his personality but his love language is words of affirmation. Now don't get me wrong, he's also affectionate. He flirts and touches me continuously. But he didn't always speak my language, so there was conflict. I wanted quality time outside the walls of our home. His definition of quality time is everyone at home chilling, watching a favorite show; but there was no engagement, conversation (unless it was about the show) or real connection. My love language is quality time, but I love the real engagement. I want to go out to dinners and have amazing conversations and laughter. I would rather meet up with you and engage with you rather than phone calls. I love to experience new things, exciting places, be amongst the crowds while not being the center of attention. I love creating new memories with my loved ones.

I've personally held people in bondage to my perception and my expectations, instead of responding to them in their own love language. If I felt like a person wasn't giving back to me what I gave out, after a while, I would first bring it to their attention. If they didn't change immediately, I would get a little bitter and withhold my affections altogether. Instead of giving it to God and allowing him to work on their hearts, I tried to fix them with my actions because surely they would miss how awesome I am and would come running back asking for my forgiveness. NOT! That didn't happen.

1. I wasn't operating out of the greatest commandment of all which is LOVE.

2. Not only was I not operating out of Love, I was unknowingly using manipulation to get my way, which is a form of emotional witchcraft. It's one of Satan's tactics he uses when imposing his will on human will, emotions, behaviors, or circumstances to make people do what they would not usually do.

I am also guilty of putting God in my own love language box. I have been serving, paying my tithes and offerings faithfully since I truly began my walk with Christ. I was also praying and reading His Word on a consistent basis. We have sown into people's lives, given to the homeless, etc. These are all my works towards Him, but I felt like when I needed Him, He was not there for me according to my timeframe. As I grew spiritually in my Christian walk, I have learned that God does not respond to temper tantrums, demands, pleas or plans that are not in accordance to His will and time frame. I've also learned that during my wait, it truly does perfect me, and it makes my character more like His.

During these times I have learned to stand on His word. "Where can I go from Your Spirit? Or where can I flee from Your presence? If I ascend to heaven, You are there; If I make my bed in Sheol, behold, You are there. If I take the wings of the dawn, If I dwell in the remotest part of the sea, Even there your hand will lead me, And Your right hand will lay hold of me. If I say, 'Surely the darkness will overwhelm me, and the light around me will be night,' Even the darkness is not dark to you, and the night is as bright as the day Darkness and light are alike to You"(Psalm 139:7-12). This tells me that He will never leave me nor forsake me, and even in my darkest, loneliest hours, He is right there beside me, loving on me and providing my every need.

God is calling us to slow down, sit down and be like Mary. Know the value and benefit of sitting at Jesus's feet. Most of us are like Martha, busy serving, doing the works of a good Christian, a friend, a spouse, mother, daughter, but never taking the time to just sit and spend that quality time with him. "Now while they were on their way, Jesus entered a village [called Bethany], and a woman named Martha welcomed Him into her home. She had a sister named Mary, who seated herself at the Lord's feet and was continually listening to His teaching. But Martha was very busy and distracted with all of her serving responsibilities; and she approached Him and said, "Lord, is it of no concern to You that my sister has left me to do the serving alone? Tell her to help me and do her part." But the Lord replied to her, "Martha, Martha, you are worried and bothered and anxious about so many things; but only one thing is necessary, for Mary has chosen the good part [that which is to her advantage], which will not be taken away from her" (Luke 10:38-42).

Thinking back when my husband and I got married. I was 20 years old and he was 24 years old. If we only knew then what we know now. All those fights and silent treatments could have been avoided. In courtship, we were the perfect match! His focus was to please me, he courted me, we studied each other always looking and searching for ways to please each other.

Our first year was bliss, we continued the courtship, but something changed in our second year. "REAL LIFE" crept in, and we started to see each other's flaws and didn't like what we saw. I was so full of hidden insecurities that ultimately came to the surface. I often operated out of rejection when he would want to spend a little more time with his friends than I wanted him to. Because his job required him to work 12 hours a day; sometimes 6 to 7 days a a week, felt like his downtime should have been spent with me, not his friends. In my mind, he was putting his friends before me, and that would cause me to lash out with my words. For a person whose primary love language is affirmations, that was a recipe for disaster. My husband on the other hand, would act unforgiving and give me the silent treatment. When he withheld his affections and his distance, it would make me feel even more insecure and feel rejected at times. Remember my primary love language is quality time that fed my feelings of rejection. We were like an atomic bomb waiting to be lit.

We bought our first home a year later and now we have this beautiful home. However, because of my husband's working hours, my mother-in-law and I immediately started to paint, trying to make this house our home, with our own identity. However, because of the space we were in, and all of our repressed feelings, it finally blew and of all days, it happened to be on Valentine's Day. After a heated discussion, I ended up leaving and moving in with his parents. Devastated and misplaced, I left my brand new home that I prayed for. Now, I'm living in someone's guest room but little did I know, that was a pivotal point in my Christian walk.

When I tell you the support and love of your church family is beyond important, and can get you through the worst of times, believe it. My Pastor Steve Hayes and his wife Par spoke into my life, prayed for me, with me, and corrected me in love. My mother and father in-love were supportive and never tried to deter me one way or another. They didn't take sides, they were on, "the what's right side." The first time we separated, I was consumed with getting my marriage back. I would drive by the house and see if he was home or if he had anybody at the house at random times of the day and night when I wasn't at work. My marriage and husband consumed my prayers; text messages and calls were continuous. I would show up at his job and leave cards and flowers on his car. I was embarrassed because when we announced we were getting married, I had people in my ear telling me "You're not ready. You are going to be the cause of your marriage failing. You need to wait till you're about 35 years old." So I was determined that they weren't going to be right. My marriage was going to make it. I was going to be happy.

So after about a month of counseling, Charles and I gave it another try. But absolutely NOTHING changed.

NOTHING!!! I was still the same girl who was wounded, who spoke my mind without regard to his feelings in the spirit of "telling it like it is" and "keeping it real." He also was the same man that was unforgiving and bitter. So once again, I was moving into my in-laws' house; even more broken and defeated, so I thought. Little did I know, this time would be different. I got before God and really sought Him for my healing and my breakthrough. I became like Mary and sat before Jesus' feet and allowed Him to speak my love languages. I stopped praying for my husband and focused on my healing. I felt the true meaning of Psalm 91:1, "Those who live in the shelter of the Most High will find rest in the shadow of the Almighty."

During this time, I truly learned there is a place only God can dwell. He preserves some spaces in your heart just for Him that NO MAN, WOMAN, OR ANYTHING CAN OCCUPY. There will always be a void that only He can fill. I learned that God does speak your ultimate love language. During this time, I allowed God to heal my spirit and soul. I was no longer in fear of failure. I could truly care less of what people would say if my marriage didn't make it because I truly gave myself and my marriage to God. I put it all on the altar. After both of us received counseling, correction and prayer, we gave our marriage yet another shot. I am so happy to say that we are still together, twelve years later!

In most instances, people rarely consider applying the five love languages to relationships other than their spouses. But, I've found that our daily relationships play an important part in our daily lives. It's so important to pick our friendships carefully. That's because a fake friend can cause more damage than your enemies. In Proverbs 18:24, the bible says, "One who has unreliable friends soon comes to ruin, but there is a friend who sticks closer than a brother." In this passage, I believe God is telling us the importance of friendships and it describes two types of friends.

A friend does not steal or manipulate your identity. If you have to change or mask your identity for their comfort, that's a strong sign that you are not in a good relationship/ friendship. There are several times that God himself is giving us warnings through discernment or physical signs in our body that something about this person and situation isn't quite right. We might not always physically see the issues, but in our inner being, we know something is there. There are always signs. No one can hide their true self for too long.

That's not to say there aren't personality traits, personal flaws and environmental influences causing a person to act the way they act. That doesn't mean they mean you harm or they're not genuine. There are times where we have to apply grace in the same manner we want someone to apply grace for our own short comings. This is not a cookie cutter application where you are on a witch hunt and try to make someone fit into your five love languages mold. This is just a guide to help you learn to put more effort into the all relationships in your life that are beneficial and good for you.

Scripture says there is a friend who sticks closer than a brother. Now, that's the friend we want to cherish, nurture and invest in. The Bible clearly gives us guidelines for our love walk. "Love is patient, love is kind. It does not envy, it does not boast, it is not proud. It does not dishonor others, it is not self-seeking, it is not easily angered, it keeps no record of wrongs. Love does not delight in evil but rejoices with the truth. It always protects, always trusts, always hopes, always perseveres. Love never fails. But where there are prophecies, they will cease; where there are tongues, they will be stilled; where there is knowledge, it will pass away" (1 Corinthians 13:4-8). Out of this list, my favorite or I feel like my strongest attribute is, "Love always Perseveres. Love never fails." For most of my life, it seems as if my life has been a revolving door. People come, people go. It felt like any little thing could derail every relationship. It caused me to go into self-protection mode where I wouldn't let anyone get close. I built the Great Wall of China around my heart and in many ways to my detriment.

When I started dating my husband, he finally persuaded me to meet my mother in love. I remember going into her home with a "lets get this over with attitude" and I remember looking into her bright happy sunset eyes, and her welcoming smile. In my head, my perception was she seemed like a nice person, but.....Nobody is actually that nice. I laugh at it now, but I remember her continuously walking towards me to make conversation. All I could think was this lady was all in my personal space. I was so uncomfortable that I bumped into this big clock in the hallway trying to nonchalantly get away from her. Little did I know, God would prove my favorite trait of perseverance through her.

During this time, I was looking for a church home. My husband suggested I check out his mom's new church. I grew up Baptist and this was the very first Non-denominational church that I had ever attended. I begged my roommate to come with me, so she did. The first time I attended, the Pastor singled me out and gave me a word of Prophesy and told me that in 6 months, my life would be completely changed. At the time, I was going out for Tyra Banks' America's Next Model auditions, so I thought I was going to win the competition and be famous traveling the world showing everyone who ever doubted me I made it. HA! So instead, 6 months later I was married, in leadership at church, working a regular 9 to 5. Not the change I expected, but exactly what I needed. During this time, I was slowly warming up to my mother-in-love, but I still had my reservations. I was just waiting until my husband's mother showed her true colors because I didn't care what anyone said, I believed Jesus could not give her this much joy all the time.

Victory Church was having a women's conference called, "Beautiful." My mother-in-love paid for my ticket and I acted so uncaring and nonchalant that she called me on it. So I wouldn't sit with her at lunch; which she also paid for. I hurt her feelings and I acted like I didn't care, so she called me an Ice Princess. When she said that to me, it was as if someone had dashed a bucket of ice cold water over me. That was the first time I felt convicted because at that moment, I truly felt her love and hurt. Even though I literally showed the worst part of me, she still wanted to love me and not throw me away. As time went on, she became my first spiritual mentor and friend. Even though our relationship was not understood, liked and often times come against, she believed God placed me in her life for a purpose and nothing or anyone will come between that. That was the beginning of God showing me through action that love perseveres through patience and love protects.

Parent/adult child relationships can be tricky because as children we depended on our parents completely. They fed us, clothed us and provided a roof over our heads. They were our biggest supporters and cheerleaders. They learned and studied us from infancy and they have our love language down pat. They can describe our personality, all our likes and dislikes without you saying a word. It was their duty, right? It was alright because after all, our parents were supposed to be our first example of God's love on earth, but what happens now that we are adults? Does the relationship description change? Now that we are adults, does the dynamic change from parent/provider to parent/child-friend? I believe it does because they are no longer legally responsible for us.

I believe we have an opportunity after we're grown to reverse our roles and pour back into our mother and father that raised us, loved us into the adults that we are now. Even if you had parents that weren't the greatest role models, it's an opportunity to show God's love. Love on them and go see about them. Learn and speak their love language. "Honor your father and mother" (Ephesians 6:2-4). This is the first commandment with a promise: If you honor your father and mother, "things will go well for you, and you will have a long life on the earth."

I have learned several things about relationships and people throughout my life. Here are five:

1. No one is perfect but God. People will hurt you, disappoint you with some being done unconsciously and some on purpose. We have to make sure we treat them right so our hearts can remain pure and clean. When we go to God in prayer, we have the confidence that God hears us because our hearts aren't muffled being unforgiving and having strife. "Work out our salvation with fear and trembling, for God is working in you, giving you the desire and the power to do what pleases him"(Philippians 2:12-13).

2. I have learned that grace is a large part of love. Not everyone deserves our forgiveness, or even wants our forgiveness. They may demonstrate it by repeating the same bad behaviors towards us. However, we can't lock ourselves into the prison of being unforgiving, because that is detrimental to our own spiritual health.

3. When we apply grace, WE ARE FREE!!! We can place them on the altar and let God handle it, and we can walk in peace. I have learned to be okay with people's personalities and their stuff. I have learned to not take everything personal, and their issues aren't always about me.

4. When a person lashes out or treats me in such a way that rubs me wrong, I have quieted the voices of my past that said I am the problem. I no longer associate myself with being the cause of their problems and I also leave myself open to Gods correction.

5. The greatest lesson of all is Love, which is a choice, not a feeling. I love this passage because as we throw the word LOVE around so much, we sometimes lose the meaning and its importance. Without love, there's no hope. Without hope, it's hard to operate in faith. Without faith, it's impossible to please God.

I believe God gave us the recipe for living a fulfilled life. I would caution you as you move forward in love throughout your life to not leave any of the key ingredients out. The key ingredients are Faith, Hope and Love. "And now these three remain: faith, hope and love. But the greatest of these is love" (1 Corinthians 13:13).

Ruby Belcher

Ruby Belcher is professional hair stylist and make-up artist who touches the lives and souls of many in establishing a deeper more meaningful relationship with Christ. Owner of "Destiny Beauty Bar", she uses her abilities to catapult women into understanding their true worth and using their talents as a means to make impact. The duality of her expertise in hair and make-up allows Ruby to serve alongside celebrity hair and make-up artists earning recognition as one of the Top make-up artists and hair stylist in Dallas 2014 – 2015 by Voyage Dallas.

Ruby's artistic capabilities have casted her to work with some of the top videographers, photographers, and film makers within North Texas. She's deemed as a successful entrepreneur who exemplifies the meaning of servant leadership. Her success is directly attributed to her innate ability to influence those around her in knowing and doing better. Noted as one of the top stylists to watch, Ruby uses her platform to push others towards their God given purpose.

A member of Word of Truth Family Church, Ruby humbly serves as an Armor Bearer and is under the leadership of Pastors Eben & Sara Conner. Ruby is married to her husband and best friend Charles, and they are the proud parents of an amazing daughter, Destiny and 2 fur babies, Diamond and Seven. In her spare time, Ruby is a foodie & loves traveling as well as spending time with family and friends. To connect with Ruby for future partnerships, speaking engagements, make-up or hair services, reach out to her at *mrsbelcher34@gmail.com*.

Chapter 14

Lessons Learned in Leadership
Ann L. Esters-Stevenson

"And let us not lose heart and grow weary and faint in acting nobly and doing right, for in due time and at the appointed season we shall reap, if we do not loosen and relax our courage and faint." Galatians 6:9

"The weak can never forgive. Forgiveness is the attribute of the strong." Mahatama Gandhi

"Leader" is the root word of Leadership. The *Business Dictionary* defines leader as "a person or thing that holds a dominant or superior position within its field and is able to exercise a high degree of control or influence over others." *Merriam-Webster* defines leader as "a person who has commanding authority or influence." I have been blessed to have been deemed a leader and placed in positions of leadership all throughout my life as far as I can remember; even dating back through high school as a cheerleader captain. While puzzled, I really don't know and can't remember why I was even chosen to be the captain of our high school cheerleading squad. In my transparency, I remember being happy, but subliminally questioned, "Had they made a mistake in choosing me?" And I wondered if I just happened to be assigned to the roll by default. It puzzled me. However, one thing is for certain, throughout my entire life starting in my adolescence, it has been apparent that others identified leadership character traits which I exhibited before I could even define the term itself.

In retrospect, I believe wholeheartedly my mother instilled skills in my brothers and I which acted as a catalyst for those characteristics to be easily identifiable. The problem is even today, I may struggle in wondering how I've been blessed to have been chosen to hold various leadership positions in both my career, church, and community. Now don't get me wrong, I deem myself as a "go-getter"; but when I look back over my life as a leader, I often wonder why GOD would place me in some of the roles in which I acquired experience. I believe most people who are leaders will share in my sentiment that leadership is not all "Glitz & Glamour" and often times, there are difficult decisions which have to be made where some may be impacted, not agree with your decision, challenge you, persecute you, and in extreme cases, bully you too!

Again, don't get me wrong, leadership definitely has its perks; and fortunately for me, the good outweighs the bad. As I reflect back throughout my overall leadership experience, I think to myself, "If I'd not experienced the adversities that go along with this particular leadership role, I wouldn't have been able to leverage the experiences that were awesome." Over the course of my career, I have come to appreciate both while establishing benchmarks along the way. Both, the good and the bad helped shape me in gaining more personal, professional, and most critical, spiritual growth. While it's a blessing for others to have identified certain leadership qualities in me, the problem is that I didn't seem to identify them in myself. As a result, I sometimes found myself constantly seeking approval and validation when I didn't have to.

It's always okay to strive at becoming a better leader (notice how I didn't say "best"). The primary reason why I prefer to use the term "better" as opposed to "best" is because as a part of my experiences, it caused others to look more at: me and what I was doing, what I had, why did I have it, how did I get it, why was I the one chosen, where I lived, and what type of car I drove; as opposed to looking at themselves and saying, "I would like to become a better leader for MYSELF, so in turn I can be a better leader for those who GOD has entrusted in my care." Yes, I said those who GOD has entrusted in my care because leadership, in my opinion, lends itself to stewardship. I believe in my heart, if leaders took a more "GODLY" approach to leadership and truly understood the stewardship principle; as it relates to governing themselves throughout all interactions, it would lessen the hostility often felt in the workplace. It would open the door for more collaborative efforts as opposed to unhealthy competitiveness. It would garner positive working relationships; which have a direct, positive impact on a corporation's bottom line. It would set the foundation of trust, which is an integral part of any relationship (business or personal). Last, but not least, it would set the stage for leaders to pour into the lives of everyone around them while catapulting their overall growth and development.

While all of this seems to be a bit vague, stick with me; as I am going somewhere with this based on my own personal experiences with various people placed in positions of leadership. I'll share with you and give you a bird's eye view into my life as a leader and almost having lost my passion to lead and just wanting to throw in the towel after being in leadership for greater than 30 years. It has been through my own personal adversities with those placed in leadership positions (women in particular) that's caused me to hone into my passion for pouring into the life of any woman I come into contact with; ensuring she understands the importance of knowing GOD values her abilities, GOD values her input, GOD values her efforts, GOD values her hard work, and GOD values her as HIS own child. These are women that I truly looked up to and desired guidance through either church, business or personal relationships. In each of these relationships, I felt comfortable as I would divulge some of my own insecurities and vulnerabilities in an effort to acquire guidance. However, in retrospect, that was not always the best thing to do as particularly in business relationships, I was made to feel inadequate as it relates to emotional intelligence.

While I must say, I definitely had work to do as it related to Emotional IQ, I quickly learned there are some things that just should not be shared as it can turn around to bite you in the (&$$). I so struggled with this because I've always had a heart for people and a desire to grow in whatever role I was blessed to have. I often talk about the deep loving relationship I had throughout my entire life with my mother. While not all peaches and cream, the majority of time having spent on earth with my mother was absolutely phenomenal. I've not always had money or material possessions, yet I had something much more valuable and that's love. Growing up was a struggle with sometimes being embarrassed at "things" I didn't have. However, as I matured, especially in my walk with Christ, I learned to love the fact that I had a mother who believed in me so much. I felt as if I could conquer the world if I really wanted to and all I had to do was put in the work.

She told me something so profound in my late teenage early adult years that I seemed to have forgotten until just a few years ago. She said, "Ann, if you live off of a person's compliments, you will surely die off of their criticisms." When she told me that, it was in an effort for me to build on the foundation she'd already established as it relates to my own self-confidence and personal self-image. However, when she passed, that concept somehow got lost. Several years later, and throughout one business relationship in particular, I found myself almost obsessed with gaining validation from a leader, Jessah Belle with whom I previously had a business relationship with. My obsession started shortly after having transitioned to Jessah's area from another business unit as I was greeted with a very short welcome quickly followed by being told I have a strong personality. A few months after that, I was informed that one of our key stakeholders was alerted that I make too much money. Ironically, the amount of money I made came up shortly after I'd gotten a new car. Never mind the fact that the car I traded in was 12 years old with greater than 140K miles. I was at a loss and really didn't know how to respond in either instance because I didn't know what actually defined a person with a strong personality. I'd never heard that term used before and definitely not used when characterizing me. As it relates to money, while I am sincerely blessed by GOD to make a decent salary; I was well beneath the designated compa-ratio which I was fine with, because it gave me room to grow and improve on my skill set. I've never aspired to be "rich." Even as a child, I would tell GOD that I want to be "wealthy" because this term encompasses so much more and to me, it adds more value than just being rich. To maintain my balance and humility as a Leader, one of the Scriptures I stand on is

"But if it's only money these leaders are after, they'll self-destruct in no time. Lust for money brings trouble and nothing but trouble. Going down that path, some lose their footing in the faith completely and live to regret it bitterly ever after" (1 Timothy 6:9-10).

Well, as you can imagine, these two comments alone became successful in my planting seeds and thoughts of doubt and inadequacy. I was made to feel on several occasions that I was to be seen and not heard. I would give information or make suggestions and would utterly be ignored. However, Jude Iscariots, another person placed in a position of leadership would say the very same thing a few weeks or months later and his suggestion or statement would be met with open arms as if he'd come up with a cure for a debilitating disease. What sealed the deal and took me in a huge downward spiral was when I was tasked with doing a presentation required to be presented to our entire team and somehow Jessah was the only one giving feedback. Two other leaders and I had already presented in prior month's meetings. However, after one particular meeting, she asked myself and Jude Iscariots, who presented in that meeting to stay behind a few moments for a brief discussion. While I didn't think that she was going to specifically talk about Jude's presentation, she proceeded to tell him that his presentation was the best so far. I was stunned! In my mind, I thought to myself, "Did this idiot just say that his presentation was the best so far right here in front of me and she's never once given any feedback on mine?" Surely, you're probably wondering the same thing.

Well, hold on. I know you're also probably wondering, "Who does that?" No worries because I wondered the same thing. I could tell her comment even made Jude Iscariots feel uncomfortable because he quickly looked at me (presumably to see if I was okay) and then looked back at her slowly putting his head down. Talk about uncomfortable. Well, get a load of this! To add insult to injury, there was no apology and she even doubled downed and said, "Well it is!" Immediately after, she said that. , I can remember feeling so extremely nauseous and wanted to excuse myself, but I couldn't move. In my mind, I was asking if I could be excused to go to the restroom, but nothing would come out of my mouth. It was like I was talking, but no one could hear the words but me. I saw myself moving, but it was like I was cemented to the chair. I felt invisible. I felt horrible. After the meeting, I remember going to the restroom and practically dry heaving because I needed to get whatever was deposited in me, OUT!

It wasn't until I learned that she didn't have the best relationship with her parents (particularly her mother)and that she had experienced her third or fourth divorce, that I began to pray for and have compassion for her. Her mother didn't want her and as cruel as it seems, someone told her that and I believe that would have been traumatizing to find out at any age. Her mother could go weeks without speaking to her especially if she was angry. Yes, I said that I began to pray for her. That very night before I went to bed, I told God, "If treating me badly will get her (and Jude) closer to Christ, then I will be the sacrifice." I thought of us as Hannah and Peninnah. Peninnah tormented Hannah. But because of Hannah's obedience and love for God, she found favor. Plus, I knew that even though I didn't like her, the Bible commands me to love her. And as my Pastor would say, "Sometimes you have to love the Hell out of them." Now, often times, even loving her was hard and it showed only because I am not perfect and I didn't handle every antagonistic situation like Jesus would. It was in those moments, I was simply tired of the bullshit.

However, soon after I would reflect on the fact that I was blessed to have a PHENOMENAL relationship with my mother and my father. They loved me unconditionally and a pack of wild horses couldn't keep my mother from speaking to or emotionally abusing me for 30 seconds, let alone weeks at a time. My father loved him some me and believed in and allowed me to be me while never comparing my strengths or my weaknesses to that of my siblings. This was not her experience and it had to hurt her when her dad would compare her to her siblings as a means to get her to do better, but it only promoted unhealthy competition and resentment which filtered over into her career. My father honed in on my personal strengths as a leader, and helped me to navigate through my weaknesses; which to most can often be deemed as strengths (passionate, loving, loyal, cautious, analytical, compassionate, giving, etc.). Again, while I didn't have many "material" things, I was blessed to be a recipient of "L O V E" and "T I M E," which are the most valuable assets any parent can give their children. Also, after having failed dating relationships, I've been blessed by GOD to have a loving relationship with my husband who, next to GOD, loves me like no other. While marriages aren't perfect, at the end of the day, I know next to GOD, he has my back, my front, and my sides, and the fight to go with it (need be).

While heavy on my path to forgiveness, I had another encounter with the same leader where she conducted a Diversity & Inclusion exercise where there was a series of questions asked of all of her direct reports to include managers. While another colleague and I were eating lunch, she came over to briefly chat. In my head, I thought, "Oh Lordt! Why in the H E Double Hockey Sticks is she over here while we're trying to eat?" In conversation, she specifically said that she "did not" ask who graduated from college and what degrees they may hold because she didn't want to make Jude feel bad for not acquiring his. By this time, I have the most puzzled look on my face and I am thinking to myself, "Now GOD, I know you told me to forgive and I am truly working on this compassion piece; but, did YOU just hear what I heard?" I said, "GOD, did she just discount the fact that I worked my A$$ off to get my degree and she has the audacity to minimize my hard work and efforts?" "OK GOD! You playin' and you got jokes today!" By this time, I knew in my heart that there was no way she even remotely valued me, my efforts, my experience (both in corporate America and church), or my entire existence. However this time, it was like déjà vu.

My colleague, who was sitting with me, looked over at me (because she knew I had my degree); she quickly looked over at Jessah and slowly put her head down. Again, there are two unsuspecting people placed in yet another uncomfortable position. A position where she (inadvertently or not) attempted to make me feel less than, invaluable and one who has nothing to contribute even though this was "supposed" to be an inclusive exercise; wherein my training, it should set a platform for us to embrace our differences promoting a more "cohesive" environment. So let's just say this…I'm not going to go into the "initial" thoughts that came to my mind because they were not good at all and I am almost positive my thoughts contained a few curse words. What I will go into is the importance of the huge lesson I learned right after I shook away the images of all of the garden tools, female dogs, and cows that had popped into my head.

I remained calm and silently began to pray. I learned that it is best to come to the realization and conclude that while several people are placed in a position of leadership, that doesn't make them a true leader. It was okay because it caused me to take a deeper look at my own leadership capabilities and some of the mistakes I'd made throughout my career. It prompted me to go back to the basics of what I learned in having to navigate through any difficult situation. I had to fast for my breakthrough. I had to fast so that God could give me clarity on exactly what He wanted me to do as it relates to my career. You see, slowly throughout this journey, I lost my passion to lead not only due to these specific instances, but how toxic the environment had become. My desire to lead in the workplace started to deteriorate. I knew for certain I didn't want to be deemed as someone who was just arbitrarily placed in a position of leadership because I talked a good game or had experience in specific areas. I truly wanted to be the leader that God knew I was and could be, given the right leader for myself as well as the right conditions to thrive. Coupled with prayer, I knew I also had to put some work in and it started with my researching the definition of leaders and all things attributable to leadership. I made note of positive characteristics of other leaders that I could adopt, mirror and practice.

Throughout my praying, I also fasted (because I've been raised to do both, especially when you want to hear from GOD). As I fasted, GOD dropped in my spirit that I needed to invest in myself and in my career by consulting a Life/Success Coach/Mentor that could get me to the next level spiritually. I was like, "What GOD? I need a Career Coach, not a Life or Success Coach! Are you kidding me?" This is because I often have those back and forth conversations with GOD as I am trying to make sense of what He is asking me to do. I'll just tell you: when it doesn't make sense, move forward anyway, in total and complete trust that GOD will lead the way and know that there is an expected end which has already been planned. You don't have to have all of the details and it pleases HIM when your faith kicks in so that you move forward not knowing who, what, when, where, or how. So that's what I did.

I actually consulted with two women who exude the characteristics of a great leader. I can tell you that not only do I owe where I am today to GOD, I also know that GOD strategically placed them in my life as far back as 2007. They have assisted in leveraging my life's experiences with those in my career, all the while focusing on the spiritual elements that would catapult me into my purpose. All I can tell you is that after having invested in myself by consulting with them, it was the best investment I ever made in my life! While they both have varying styles of delivery, each of them would pray for and with me which is essential. Their prayers alone, let me know I was dealing with women who had a direct connection to GOD and this is why they have been so successful in their relationships and businesses. They each hold characteristics that I have emulated throughout this phase of my own life as a Mentor and Coach. One of those characteristics includes humility. I learned that humility is power under control. As a result, my interactions, as well as my view of the interaction and the person, changed. I now tap into the power of positivity when I am faced with an adverse work situation.

Another characteristic includes grace. I re-learned that no matter how I am treated by anyone, I should always handle the situation with both dignity and grace. Our former First Lady of the United States, Michelle Obama, coined it best, "When they go low, we go high." This quote is so relatable to me. So as I would often hear of the damaging conversations that Jessah or Jude would have about me, I would continue to smile, speak, and maintain civility when in their presence. Obedience is yet another characteristic that each of these women possess and it too has set the foundation for my growth. While this is something that I struggled with in the past throughout my personal life, I really do understand that obedience unlocks the doors to opportunities designed by GOD to get me to my "Next Next." Through my obedience, I have learned that while I have not been the perfect leader, I now have yet another opportunity to get it right. This time, I am walking in what GOD has destined for me, as opposed to what I thought would come from leaders whom I trusted had my best interests at heart.

Yet another characteristic they possess that I believe most of us excessively struggle with is forgiveness, and this is yet another one that I had to quickly incorporate into my regimen every single day. I believe my struggle solely correlated to trust or the lack thereof, that I held on to based upon the repetitiveness of the offenses. What I learned is, even though my mouth said that I'd forgiven her, my mind and my heart had not. Ultimately, I was a hypocrite. I re-learned after reflecting on a conversation that my Pastor's wife held with a group of women at Bible study. She said something to the reference of, "You know that you have truly forgiven a person when you place yourself in the same situation for them to hurt/offend you again." While I agree with this statement wholeheartedly, after the repeated offenses I experienced, I found it difficult to place myself in the very same situation over and over again. I asked GOD to open the door for me to deeply hone into my passion so that I could more easily glide into my purpose. In that, I learned that it was healthier for me, in order to love this leader as GOD commands me to do, I had to do it at a safe distance. I came across a quote by an unknown author that I hold near and dear to my heart, "Forgiveness is not about letting someone off the hook for their actions, but freeing ourselves of the negative energies that bind us to them."

Last, but definitely not least, the final characteristic that I strive to emulate from my Business Mentor & Coach is compassion. While I started down this road, in my mind, the offenses just got to be too much. However, I had to come to the realization that her life's experiences have shaped the human being that she's become and just because my life's experiences are polar opposite, it doesn't give me the right to think of her in anyway other than who GOD created her to be. Additionally, for me to think highly of myself in comparison to her is downright sinful. In order for me to move forward in my passion for pouring into the lives of other women and making sure they feel worthy, valued, loved, appreciated, honored, respected, and all the rest, I have no choice but to exhibit compassion to those women who have been placed in positions of leadership and lacked humility, thus abusing their position. As a Christian, I've been charged to meet them where they are and realize it's not fair for me to place "my" expectations on them based on where "I" think they should be as it relates to leadership. God has them on their path and I need to focus on staying in my own lane and the path He has for me.

As I close and as crazy as this might sound, I am really thankful for what I endured. You see, all of this was a part of God's plan for my life & while it didn't feel good when I was experiencing it, I realize that instead of being bitter about what happened, it's been nothing but a blessing in disguise. This one experience was the icing on the cake relative to all of my adverse experiences. By far it was the worst, yet it's in the process of yielding me my biggest blessing. If not for what I endured, my PassionForPouring Facebook Group would not have been birthed and I would not be as zealous in pouring into the lives of others. We are well on our way to having thousands of members. So, I thank God for her and you should too. Chest out, chin up and thank God for anyone who tries to break you because take it from me...your blessing is on its way.

I'll leave you with 5 Lessons Learned in Leadership which helped to equip me in being able to view the adverse experiences I've encountered with leaders in my past, and add critical ministerial components to make sure that I continue by any means necessary, to move forward in what GOD is calling me to do in order to pour into the life of someone else who has similar experiences.

Lessons Learned

1. **Start making what GOD is doing in and through you (right here and right now) bigger than what others have done to you!**

   "So, what do you think? With God on our side like this, how can we lose? If God didn't hesitate to put everything on the line for us, embracing our condition and exposing himself to the worst by sending his own Son, is there anything else he wouldn't gladly and freely do for us? And who would dare tangle with God by messing with one of God's chosen? Who would dare even to point a finger?" Romans 8:31-34 The Message (MSG)

2. **Start believing in yourself and your own GOD given capabilities as opposed to seeking the validation and approval from others who have nothing to do with your future or salvation!**

   "I will give thanks and praise to You, for I am fearfully and wonderfully made; Wonderful are Your works, And my soul knows it very well." Psalm 139:14 Amplified Bible (AMP)

3. **Start speaking to GOD as if HE is your leader and ask HIM how HE would have you to conduct yourself in order to be successful and ultimately get to the Kingdom of Heaven.**

   "And whatever you do, do it heartily, as to the Lord and not to men." Colossians 3:23 New King James Version (NKJV)

4. **Start adapting to living a life of compassion and forgiveness to break any chains or bonds which**

hold you captive preventing you from unlocking GOD given opportunities and assignments.

"Be kind and helpful to one another, tender-hearted [compassionate, understanding], forgiving one another [readily and freely], just as God in Christ also forgave you." Ephesians 4:32 Amplified Bible (AMP)

5. **Start praying for every leader you know at both the company in which you work as well as your church.**

"Now we ask you, brothers and sisters, to appreciate those who diligently work among you [recognize, acknowledge, and respect your leaders], who are in charge over you in the Lord and who give you instruction, and [we ask that you appreciate them and] hold them in the highest esteem in love because of their work [on your behalf]. Live in peace with one another. We [earnestly] urge you, believers, admonish those who are out of line [the undisciplined, the unruly, the disorderly], encourage the timid [who lack spiritual courage], help the [spiritually] weak, be very patient with everyone [always controlling your temper]. See that no one repays another with evil for evil, but always seek that which is good for one another and for all people." I Thessalonians 5:12-15 Amplified Bible (AMP)

Ann L. Esters-Stevenson

Ann L. Esters-Stevenson is an Award Winning, Best Selling Author, Influential Speaker, & Leader who is deemed a *"Woman after GOD's own heart"* & has an unyielding passion to ***"Pray it Forward"*** by pouring into the lives of other Women. Ann has greater than 30 years' Corporate Leadership experience encompassing areas of Training, Coaching, Development, & Business Continuous Improvement initiatives while having earned 2 Six Sigma Green Belt Certifications. A Diversity & Inclusion Leader, she's an advocate for promoting more diverse, inclusive, & equitable work environments through leading various Employee-Business Resource Groups.

Ann humbly serves under the Leadership of Senior Pastor, Dr. Denny D. Davis, and has been a proud member of St. John Church Unleashed since 2002. She has served in various leadership capacities as Facilitator & Coach for a mentoring & discipleship ministry for hundreds of women. Ann is a member of the Christian Women in Media Association & maintains strong philanthropic partnerships with organizations throughout the Dallas-Fort Worth Metroplex. Her passion also includes serving the underserved through both direct & indirect support of both women & children.

Ann has been both a featured guest speaker & panelist at Prairie View A&M University, as well as on several radio shows & blogs while having conducted her own faith based Women's Workshops titled, ***"Love, Life & Lessons Learned"*** focusing on empowering Women to 1st be the BEST they can be for themselves so they can be the BEST for someone else. Her workshops place a deep emphasis on the acronym **G.R.A.C.E.**, 5 Guiding Principles to utilize on a daily basis to establish a healthy mind-set.

Having earned her undergraduate degree from Texas Wesleyan University, Ann owns A.L.E.S. Consulting, LLC specializing in Coaching & Mentoring clients to operate in wholeness Spiritually, Emotionally, & Professionally. She is married to her Best Friend & Husband, Shaun, has 2 Ahhmazing *S*-Sons, & an adorable Yorkshire Terrier, Seven {007}. In her spare time, she loves to journal, shop, travel, spend time with family, and has an avid collection of crosses. Connect with Ann via her website @ *www.theannlorraine.com* to secure her for future Speaking Engagements or Women's Empowerment Workshops.

Gratiude

I would like to express my heart felt gratitude to everyone who has read, donated, or purchased my first of many book projects to come. In reading, I Pray that you have been inspired based upon the small glimpse of our lives as we all authentically shared both struggles and successes. These stories were written as a means of healing and to promote our overall purpose in strengthening the mind, body, and hearts of those we touch. I would ask and thank you in advance for providing a positive review of "Love, Life & Lessons Learned" on Amazon. Last, but not least, my Prayer is that we can remain connected through your joining my Facebook Group, "PassionForPouring" as well as follow "Passion4Pouring" on Instagram so you can continue to be encouraged to go one step further, empowered to really know your self-worth, and educated to push for positive change within yourself, others, and the world.

Ann Lorraine Esters-Stevenson

28323565R00120

Made in the USA
Columbia, SC
14 October 2018